KT-198-316

C333109539

The Contented Cook

For Richard

The Contented Cook

Fuss-free food throughout the year

XANTHE CLAY

Photography by Tara Fisher

KYLE BOOKS

Published 2012 by Kyle Books
23 Howland Street, London W1T 4AY
general.enquiries@kylebooks.com
www.kylebooks.com

10 9 8 7 6 5 4 3 2 1

ISBN 978-0-85783-023-4

Text © 2012 Xanthe Clay
Design © 2012 Kyle Books

Editor: Judith Hannam
Editorial Assistant: Laura Foster
Photographer: Tara Fisher
Designer: Jacqui Caulton
Home economy and styling: Annie Rigg
Production: Nic Jones and Gemma John
Copy editor: Stephanie Evans
Proofreader: Marilyn Inglis
Indexer: Alex Corrin

A Cataloguing in Publication record for this title is
available from the British Library.

Printed and bound by 1010 Printing International Ltd

Contents

Introduction

What makes a contented cook? Certainly not a beautiful kitchen or even a tidy one, although I admit to feeling particularly serene on the rare moments when mine is in order. Nor does one need unlimited funds, just enough to buy decent ingredients, which aren't necessarily expensive. It's not about flashy techniques either, although most of us enjoy a bit of mild showing off from time to time.

Contented cooking is about enjoying the process, the soothing qualities of stirring ingredients, the fact that some things, like cooking an onion, can't be rushed. It's getting food on the table without breaking sweat, and then eating it. For many of us it's a much needed change of focus, too, a bit of creative outlet and craftsmanship, after a day at the workplace coalface.

There's a steady rhythm to good cooking. If we eat three times a day, that means heading for the kitchen once, twice, thrice a day, week in week out. There's the shopping, the chopping, the ladling, and the meals marked by the seasons, the ingredients and the feasts and festivals of the year. Lose that rhythm and it will become a chore.

These are some of my favourite contented recipes, the ones I turn to again and again. Because, in cookery, repetition is a good thing, soothing, like rereading a great novel. I learn something new every time.

And remember, that whatever the flashy television shows would like us to believe, this is a way of life, not a competition. Anyway, if you are making fresh food at home, you have already won. So enjoy it for itself. It's about making food that pleases people, but also, most importantly, the cook.

Early Spring

Spring is for cooks. With weather that can most optimistically be called challenging, early spring needs all the help it can get in the kitchen front, and I love it. Now, my friends, we get to show our mettle, to transform the limited range of fresh fruit and vegetables into comforting meals. In fact, it's a time for real cooking.

Without the voluptuous charms of strawberries or pumpkins or cherries to brighten the chill months, it takes ingenuity to avoid monotony. Few of the ingredients available early in the year make a meal in the way that an outstandingly good tomato with a sprinkling of salt can be the focus of a summer lunch. So get to the stove.

Not that dishes need to be complicated or difficult. A pot of cabbage gently cooked with strips of streaky bacon and finely chopped onion takes little more than half an hour to put on the table and is savoury and comforting. Fish and broccoli spiked with chilli and anchovy requires just five ingredients and is as complex flavoured and delicious as any restaurant dish.

Still not enticing enough? Now is the time to raid the greengrocer for pineapples, mangoes, passionfruit and papaya, their citrus hues clear and bright. Their lush, rich flavours are the yin to the yang of brassicas, roots and shoots.

Just as I begin to look covetously at the bags of imported salads in the supermarket, the young green leaves appear. There are foraged weeds and herbs, wild garlic and tender infant nettles for soups, chickweed and tiny lime leaves for salads. The buds are appearing on the fruit trees and summer is on the horizon.

Leeks

Leeks are alliums, like onions but more refined in taste. To be fair, onions are the ones to choose when you want caramelisation, so only onions will do for French onion soup or Alsatian onion tart. And onions roast better than leeks too, being softer, sweeter and juicier. But leeks have a more delicate, complex flavour, that makes them a better choice for most soups or casseroles. They are damn fine on their own too, especially if you can find the slender babies. For any of my recipes, you can use the white and the light to lime-zest green part. Peel away the dark bits and any shrivelled or dry layers. Even the very top is often useable underneath its forest-green mantle.

How to clean them

Leeks can be grubby customers, with all those layers to harbour whatever the rain and wind drives into them. If you are using them whole, trim them hard and place the tops directly under the cold tap, blasting away the dirt. It's easier to clean them once they are sliced or chopped. Put them in a bowl and run the cold tap over them until the bowl is full. Give them a vigorous stir around, jiggling and splashing. Then let them soak for a few minutes, so any earth and dust can sink to the bottom of the bowl. Scoop the cleaned leeks off the top of the water with your hands, and you are ready to go.

Leeks à la Grècque

When my mother made this for seventies dinner parties, it was the epitome of Elizabeth David-style food chic. Slippery soft, sweet-sour leeks are still fantastic and this is a fine way to celebrate the tender baby leeks, every bit as good as asparagus in their own way. Some slices of ham, cooked or air-dried, go well alongside the leeks. Or you can pretty them up with a little mimosa of egg – just arrange the dressing-drenched leeks on a serving dish, and rub a hard-boiled egg yolk through a sieve over the top.

Serves 4 as a starter

12–16 baby leeks, no thicker than your finger, washed and trimmed

Handful of flat-leaf parsley, chopped

FOR THE VINAIGRETTE

1 tablespoon wine vinegar (red or white)

1 tablespoon grain mustard

1 tablespoon Dijon mustard

Pinch of sea salt

5 tablespoons olive oil

Steam the baby leeks until just tender. Meanwhile whisk together the vinegar, mustards and a generous pinch of sea salt. Whisk in the olive oil to make a yellow ochre, brown-speckled emulsion.

Arrange the hot leeks in a container that holds them snugly, pour over the dressing and leave to cool. Serve on a platter scattered with the parsley.

Cock-a-Leekie Soup

This Scottish classic looks as if it has too few ingredients to be good. But somehow the long slow cooking melts the leeks to make an unctuous soup, with rich sweetness coming from the prunes. The key thing here is that, after the initial boil, the soup should simmer gently. Cook it too hard and the chicken will be tough. This soup is filling. Follow it with cheese and bread, and a bowl of apples.

Serves 4 generously as a main course

4 chicken legs, skin on

1kg leeks, sliced and washed (including the green parts)

12 pitted prunes

Salt and freshly ground black pepper

Put the chicken pieces in a pan with 3 litres of water and bring to the boil. Use a ladle to skim off the white scum that comes to the surface and reduce the heat to a gentle simmer. Cook for 30 minutes, then add half the leeks and the prunes, plus a couple of fat pinches of salt and a grinding of pepper. Simmer for 1½ hours, then add the rest of the leeks, and cook for a further 30 minutes.

Taste and add more salt and pepper as necessary. Scoop out the chicken legs, leave to cool slightly, then remove the skins and throw them away. Pull the flesh from the bones, shredding it slightly, and return to the pan. Heat through gently, and serve.

Baked Penne with Leeks, Mustard and Bacon

Baked pasta is irresistible, bubbling and golden. This one's creamy and savoury with a bit of punch from the mustard, and slippery sweetness from the leeks. Use any small pasta shape you like, although I prefer the tubes of penne, which seem to add lightness to the dish.

Serves 4–6

225g streaky bacon, chopped

4 leeks, sliced and washed

1 tablespoon Dijon mustard

200ml crème fraîche

340g penne

1 thick slice of white bread
 (a day or two old, ideally)

100g grated Gruyère or
 Parmesan

1 tablespoon butter

Salt and freshly ground
 black pepper

FOR THE WHITE SAUCE

2 tablespoons butter

2 tablespoons plain flour

600ml milk

Preheat the oven to 220°C/gas mark 7.

To make the white sauce, melt the butter and stir in the flour. Cook for 2 minutes, then whisk in the milk until smooth. Leave to simmer very gently while making the rest of the dish.

Fry the bacon in a large pan until the fat runs, then add the leeks and cook until soft. Stir in the mustard, crème fraîche and white sauce, then taste and season with salt and pepper.

Meanwhile, put the pasta to boil in a huge pan of boiling salted water. While the pasta is cooking, whizz the bread to crumbs in a food-processor. Mix the crumbs with the cheese.

Once the pasta is just fractionally underdone, drain it and add to the creamy leek mixture. Tip the lot into a large gratin dish and scatter over the cheese and crumbs. Dot with butter and bake for 10–15 minutes until browned.

Brassicas

Let's hear it for cabbage. It's beautiful, to start with, a huge rose with outer leaves curling like petals around the spherical heart. There are the seersucker leaves of Savoy cabbage, the dusky maroon of red cabbage, the pink-tinged charm of January King, and countless others. Even if some soulless supermarket or greengrocer has trimmed away the outside ruff, the tight football of goodness that remains has a satisfying neatness.

Cabbages aren't the most glamorous of vegetables I grant you, with neither the glitz of red peppers nor the charm of asparagus – more Harrison Ford than Brad Pitt. But when the weather is grey, the trees are bare and you haven't seen a homegrown lettuce for months, cabbage provides a green fix that's far better than a bag of pallid, imported rocket.

A pile of steaming leaves is the cold season's answer to salad. Cabbage can be braised in a soup or sliced into a salad with an appealingly nutty, peppery flavour: brassicas are, like that rocket, part of the mustard family. They need a little care to prepare, but then what doesn't?

Revel in the variety. The cabbage cousins are all good eating too. There are the pointed spring cabbages, which like the Tin Man have no heart but are sweet and tender for all that, and need only turning in hot butter for a minute or two.

Curly kale is another matter; coarse and ferric, it needs bludgeoning into submission and a virtue made of that robustness. Best of all are the green rosettes of sprout tops, trimmed from the end of the sticks of Brussels sprouts before harvest. (In fact, they are better than sprouts, with a gentler flavour and softer texture; a treat if you can find them.)

Then there are the flowerhead brassicas, composite flowers, in fact; the clean white curds of cauliflower, the strange whorls of day-glo green romanesco, calabrese and purple sprouting broccoli. Beware of overcooking them, as the delicate flowerheads disintegrate easily but that said, aim for tender rather than crunchy. Eating them shouldn't be a battle.

All these do well with strong flavours, the punch of chilli, of mustard or vinaigrette. No need to cosset them or be reverential. These are the big boys of the vegetable world.

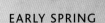

Cauliflower with Parsley and Dijon Mustard

The white curds of cauliflower are watery and bland if over-cooked, mild and nutty when cooked right, which is to say tender rather than crunchy, but retaining a little bite. It is good dressed up like this with a spunky mustard butter and lots of parsley. Serve it simply with roast meat.

Serves 3–4 as a side dish

½ cauliflower, split into florets

1 tablespoon butter

2 tablespoons Dijon mustard

Small bunch of flat-leaf parsley, leaves only, chopped

Put the cauliflower in a pan with the butter, half the mustard and enough water to reach a depth of 1cm. Cover tightly and cook for about 5 minutes, until the cauliflower is tender. Remove the lid and raise the heat to boil off the excess water. Stir in the rest of the mustard and the parsley, and then serve.

Broccoli and Boconccini Salad

A good whack of chilli and garlic with some peppery olive oil make a great foil for the broccoli in this superfood-packed salad. Eat it warm or cold, omitting the garlic and adding some lemon zest if you're taking it to the office for lunch.

Serves 2 as a main or 4 as a starter

400g purple sprouting broccoli (more if it needs a lot of trimming)

1 mild chilli, thinly sliced

1 garlic clove, halved lengthways and thinly sliced

4 tablespoons olive oil

100g boconccini (mozzarella pearls), drained

2 tablespoons capers in vinegar, drained

Salt and freshly ground black pepper

Steam the broccoli until barely tender, and still with a bit of bite to it. If you are planning to eat the salad cold, then immerse the broccoli immediately in a bowl of iced water to chill it, then drain.

Mix the cold or still warm broccoli with all the other ingredients. Season carefully with salt and pepper.

Cabbage with Bacon

A cabbage supper sounds like school dinners but in fact it is fabulous comfort food, the kind that makes me feel happy and cosseted when cooked like this with some good bacon and a little onion. It's nourishing and satisfying on its own, but makes a smart bed for grilled white fish too, the sort of dish modern-rustic restaurants love, pearly white flakes and green peppery brassica. In that case I'd spoon some soft, cream-enriched mashed potato alongside.

Serves 3–4

3–4 rashers smoked streaky bacon, chopped

1 large onion, or a handful of shallots, chopped

1 large Savoy or January King cabbage, or a couple of pointed spring cabbages, tough stems removed, finely sliced

Salt and freshly ground black pepper

Fry the bacon in a large pan until the fat runs. Add the onion and continue cooking until the onion is soft and translucent (at least 10 minutes).

Add the cabbage and a sprinkling of salt, stir briefly and cover. You shouldn't need any water if the lid is a good fit.

Cook very gently, stirring occasionally, until the cabbage wilts. As soon as it is softly chewy, but not soggy, taste and season with pepper and salt if it needs it. Serve hot.

A little note on breadcrumbs

Stop! Don't chuck out that old bread – as long as it isn't mouldy, it's perfect, better than fresh, for one of the most useful ingredients of the kitchen, breadcrumbs. It's worth making both kinds, dry and fresh:

Dry breadcrumbs are the fine, powdery kind. Slice old bread thinly, cutting off the crusts if it is artisanal bread, which get too hard. Lay on a baking tray to dry further overnight or put it in a low oven to toast lightly – you want to avoid sneaky soft layers in the middle of the slice. Put in a plastic bag and bash with a mallet or the base of a saucepan to reduce them to large crumbs. Then, if the bread is not too hard (sadly, the better the bread the harder it tends to go) grind it to fine crumbs in a food-processor. Otherwise, pound in a pestle and mortar. Either way, the counsel of perfection is to sieve the crumbs before packing them in well-sealed plastic bags and storing them in the freezer. They can be used straight from the freezer.
Use them for: Pangrattato and coating just about anything before frying. To make a proper *pané* coating, dip the ingredient in seasoned flour, then beaten egg, then breadcrumbs before shallow- or deep-frying.

Fresh breadcrumbs are the soft, coarser looking kind. Cut the crusts off your old bread (they will spoil the texture). White bread is best, brown is fine, but granary kinds with bits of grain in are generally best left for dry breadcrumbs. Whizz the soft middle to crumbs in a food-processor. Pack into plastic bags, seal well and freeze. Use straight from the freezer.
Use them for: coating ingredients before frying, as for the dry breadcrumbs. An essential ingredient in Queen's Pudding, and many stuffings, as well as for *pangrattato* and the grilled asparagus on page 56.

Purple Sprouting Broccoli with Anchovy and Chilli Butter

Anchovies add a deeply savoury heft to the butter here, turning simple steamed broccoli into a dish I'd happily eat by itself for supper. Some simply cooked fish would be excellent alongside too. Even if you don't like anchovies, you'll love this. It's not fishy at all, I promise – the little cured slivers melt away into the butter leaving only what the Japanese call *umami*, the fifth taste alongside sweet, salty, sour and bitter. It's what makes Parmesan cheese, soy sauce and tomatoes taste so good.

Serves 4 as a side dish or starter

50g unsalted butter

6 large anchovies in olive oil (sold in tins and jars), chopped

1 red chilli, deseeded and finely sliced

2 garlic cloves, finely chopped

300g purple sprouting broccoli, trimmed

Melt the butter in a small pan and add the anchovies and as much of the chilli as you like – there should be a definite kick to the finished sauce. Sizzle gently, stirring occasionally for a couple of minutes, until the anchovies melt into the butter. Stir in the garlic and cook for a few more seconds, then remove from the heat.

Steam the broccoli until just done. (An asparagus steamer is the pan to use, should you have one.) Toss the broccoli in the hot butter and serve.

Anchovies

A jar of anchovies in the fridge is as essential to me as a lemon in the fruit bowl. Nothing is as densely savoury as the anchovy, or as able to bring such a whack of *umami* to your cooking. So even if whole anchovies are too much for you, it would be culinary madness to miss out on the flavour-enhancing qualities of a couple of fillets melted into a sauce or a casserole. Yes, even a beef or lamb casserole – anchovy transcends the meat/fish boundaries. They break down in heat to melt invisibly into butter or oil so you won't even know they are there. Mind you, I can happily eat them straight from the can, especially the delectable, fat pink Cantabrian ones.

For cooking, my favourites are those that come neatly arranged vertically in a jar of olive oil, but salted ones are good too. They can come whole, salt crystals glittering against the silver skin, but removing the bones and innards is a simple matter of pushing your thumb into the belly cavity and pulling out the whole lot. Don't worry about the odd, hair-like bone still clinging to the fillet. All salted anchovies need rinsing to remove the salt crystals, then soaking for at least a couple of hours to reduce the salinity. Then use in the same way as anchovies in oil.

Whatever you use, don't be seduced by the silver skinned, creamy fleshed pickled anchovies arranged in cartwheels in delis. Called *bocquerones* in Spain, these vinegary specimens are for eating on bread or alone, not for cooking, and never, ever, on a Caesar salad.

Melting Kale with Green Olives and Garlic

Kale is a tricky beast. It looks stunning, exuberant like curly parsley. But, like curly parsley, it can be coarse and rough-tasting. My conversion came late when I visited the Danish chef Camilla Plum at her farm north of Copenhagen. Kale grew in magnificent plumes in her vegetable garden, and as Plum harvested the long, crinkled black-green leaves, she referred to it as Northern Cavolo Nero. This doesn't just sound far sexier, but gives a clue that with a little care, as with its Italian cousin, it can be transformed from beast to gastronomic beauty. This recipe makes the most of kale's ferric, punchy-flavoured charms, cooked slowly to softness and balanced with olives, garlic and plenty of olive oil.

Serves 4–6

1 huge head or 2 large heads of kale

6–8 tablespoons olive oil

4 fat garlic cloves, peeled and sliced

6 green olives, pitted and sliced

In a nutshell: Blanch the kale and cook it very gently for 30 minutes or more in olive oil with the garlic. Season generously and stir in the olives.

First time full instructions: Strip the frilly kale leaves from their coarse stems, pulling out any thick central veins as you go. Plunge all the leaves into a bowl of cold water and leave to soak for a few minutes, swishing them around occasionally. Lift the leaves out of the water – if the water looks very muddy, then wash the kale again.

Bring a pan of water to the boil and plunge in the washed kale. Boil for 2 minutes. Meanwhile, heat the oil gently in a large pan. Add the garlic, and heat it through, but don't let it sizzle or brown.

Drain the kale and add to the oil and garlic. Cook very gently, covered, for 30 minutes or more until it is very very tender.

Slice the olives and stir them in. Raise the heat and cook off any excess water or just leave to infuse for a few minutes before serving (a good opportunity to finish preparing the rest of the meal).

How to use it

Lovely as a side dish with any game or rich winter casserole. Pile it on sourdough toast and serve with roast pigeon.

Tip

It's vital to strip out the tough stems of the kale before cooking, but the leaves are often sold in bags, already chopped into short lengths. This makes preparation, frankly, more trouble than it's worth. Buy kale only if you can find the leaves whole.

More ways with brassicas

Caught-on-the-bottom Cabbage

Melt a good dollop of salted butter (and it does need to be butter, not oil) in a large pan. Add a sliced green cabbage or spring cabbage or brussels tops, and allow to wilt in the sizzling butter. Stir only occasionally, so the edges of the cabbage caramelise, and almost burn. Season with salt and pepper and eat as a side vegetable.

Brussels Tops

Sprout tops, lopped off the stems of Brussels sprouts are some of the finest greens you can hope to eat, gentler flavoured, sweet and generally far superior to the sprouts themselves. Wash the jolly green rosette and pull the leaves from the stems, gather them in a ball and slice through once or twice. Heat a knob of butter in a pan, add the leaves with a good sprinkling of salt and pepper. Cook, stirring every now and then, until the leaves have wilted and eat straight away.

Brussels Tops Stems

No need to throw away the stems and the tiny sproutlets attached. Slice them all (peel just the fat central stem first) and cook in butter like the leaves, but for longer, say 15 minutes, until tender. Season well and eat hot.

Cauliflower, Broccoli/Calabrese Stems

The stems are the best bit of the vegetable, sweet and nutty with a crisp texture like water chestnuts, so don't even think of throwing these away either. Peel off the tough skin – it's easiest and most efficient to do this with your fingers, removing the fibrous outer layer in strips from top to bottom, but use a small knife if it gets tiresome. Then slice the tender core into rounds. Cook in a little butter until tender or add to the steaming basket with the rest of the vegetable. Or use in a stir-fry rather than, you guessed it, water chestnuts.

Cauliflower, Romanesco or Broccoli with Pangrattato

Melt 2 tablespoons butter in a large frying pan and stir in half a teacupful of fresh dry breadcrumbs (see page 17). Cook, stirring often, until the crumbs are golden and crisp, and add a fat garlic clove, crushed, and the grated zest of ½ lemon. Season with salt and pepper, and sprinkle generously over hot steamed cauliflower, romanesco or broccoli.

Beetroot

Banish all thoughts of coarse, vinegary pickled beets. Proper beetroot is sweet, earthy and utterly delicious. It's so good for you it even turns your wee pink, which can be a little alarming for the unwary but is proof that it is rammed full of the antioxidant betanin. Its sweetness makes it good with game birds and red meat, but it is also fantastic in cold-weather salads.

Beetroot basics

Buying

Always buy beetroot in a bunch with bouncy fresh leaves still on if you can. If nothing else, it is an indication that they are freshly harvested, since the leaves wilt quickly. And you'll have the tops as a bonus vegetable (see opposite). The original Buy One Get One Free.

Storing

Once you get them home, chop off the leaves and stems and use them first (store the beets in the fridge or a cool larder). The root is dedicated to feeding the leaves, so it will pump all its goodness into them and go soft if left intact. The same is true, incidentally, of bunches of radishes or any root veg.

Baking

This is the best way of all to cook beetroot: The oven temperature isn't important – just wash and bung them in with what ever else you are cooking (above 160°C/gas mark 3). As a guide, 40 minutes or so at 190°C/gas mark 5 for golf ball-sized beets should do the trick, but exact timing depends on the size and age of the beets. When they are tender enough to be speared with a fork, leave to cool then peel off the wrinkled grey skin to reveal the dense, almost unctuous flesh.

Microwaving

If you aren't already using the oven, then this is more fuel efficient as well as faster. Wash the beetroot well and put in a microwave-proof bowl and cover with clingfilm. Microwave for 4 minutes, then check to see if they are tender. If not, cook again, checking every minute or so. Leave to cool then peel off the skin with your fingers.

Cheating

For a weeknight supper, ready-cooked vacuum-packed beetroot is pretty good, but check the pack first to ensure it has no vinegar in it. Old-fashioned greengrocers sometimes sell cooked beets too, but these have usually been cooked in cheap vinegar – or worse, vinegar substitute. Caveat emptor.

Root to tip eating – and what to do with the tops

The tops aren't a reason to buy beetroot (the roots are very much the star) and they need a little nurturing not to be coarse, but that doesn't mean they aren't worth eating.

Wash them well and chop the stems into pea pod-sized lengths. The leaves need only rough chopping. Cook the stems in hot butter for 10–15 minutes until tender. Meanwhile, plunge the leaves into a pan of boiling salted water and cook for 1 minute. Drain and squeeze dry in a tea towel.

Stir a clove or two of crushed garlic and some chopped chilli in with the stems, then add the leaves, teasing them apart and mixing well with the butter. When hot through, taste and adjust the seasoning, adding a squeeze of lemon if you like. Good with sausages or red meat.

Beetroot, Watercress and a Delicate Goats' Cheese

Here beetroot is part of a simple tumble of ingredients that makes a pretty starter or a good lunch. As with all simple assemblages, balance is key. So be careful with the dressing, which should have an almost imperceptible lift from the acidity of the sherry vinegar. The point is to match the ferric-flavoured watercress leaves with the tender sweet beetroot and the mild tang and rich creaminess of the cheese.

Serves 2 as lunch or supper with bread, 4 as a starter

4 golf ball-sized (or a little larger) beetroot, cooked and peeled

85g watercress (about 1 large bunch, once you've chopped off the coarse stems), washed

1 teaspoon sherry vinegar

Pinch of salt

3 tablespoons olive oil

50g mild goats' cheese, ideally the kind with an almost mousse-like texture, such as Ragstone

Cut the beetroot into wedges or chunks. Snip the watercress into manageable lengths. (This is especially important if you have bought it in one of those inflated pillow-packs, a tangle of long stems with tiny leaves. No one wants to struggle to jam bouncy strands of watercress into their mouth.)

Whisk the vinegar with a fat pinch of salt, then whisk in the oil. Dress the beetroot and watercress and spread it out on a serving platter. Drop teaspoonfuls (or scatter large crumbs) of the cheese over the salad. Serve straight away.

Types of goats' cheese

In recipes, goats' cheese adds heft to flavours. The more delicate fresh cheeses are best in salads, as are soft goats' curds. Look for them at farmer's markets. Older cheeses, like the chèvre logs, have a soft rind that can be grilled to a savoury brown crust, meltingly creamy beneath. (Don't leave that rind on the side of the plate, it has flavour and texture of its own.) Really hard goats' cheese, as firm as cheddar, can be grated or cubed and mixed into robust salads, but is best of all on a cheeseboard.

Beetroot and Potato Purée

A vivid magenta purée that works as both potato and vegetable. It's brilliant with roast beef, that sweet earthy flavour pointing up the mild meatiness. Alongside, tuck a posy of watercress on each plate. The bouncy dark green leaves give a fresh peppery bite, are gorgeous for mopping up gravy and get round your having to cook a green vegetable. Lazy Sunday lunch. Any leftover purée makes a great soup. Thin with stock or a mixture of stock and milk, and serve hot with a dollop of crème fraîche.

Serves 4–6

500g floury potatoes, peeled
   and cut into large chunks

500g cooked beetroot
   (see page 23)

100ml milk

Salt and freshly ground
   black pepper

TO FINISH

Crème fraîche

Butter

Cook the potatoes in plenty of boiling salted water until tender. Drain into a sieve and put the sieve back over the hot pan. Cover with a tea towel and leave to dry.

Purée the beetroot in a food-processor until really smooth.

Heat the milk in a pan and mash the potatoes in it. A mouli-légumes (or vegetable mill) is the best utensil for the job but if you are using a regular potato masher, make sure you remove all the lumps.

Stir in the puréed beetroot. Season with salt and pepper, add a good dollop each of butter and crème fraîche. Reheat, stirring in the pan, or place in a covered dish in a warm oven.

If you see goats' butter for sale, snap it up and use it for sautéeing vegetables or fish. It has only a subtle goats' cheese flavour, less sweet than ordinary cow's butter, and just enough to add an interesting complexity to savoury dishes. One point to consider. When I asked vegetarian friends what 'veggie option' they liked to be given when eating at a friend's house, the overwhelming response was, 'Anything, as long as it's not goats' cheese again.' Sometimes, it seems, you can get too much of a good thing.

Home-cured Salmon with Beetroot and Horseradish

This salmon is cured in a similar way to gravadlax, and the result has a sweet flavour too with the added bite of horseradish. It makes a brilliant alternative to smoked salmon. The beetroot isn't compulsory, but it adds flavour as well as a pretty pink edging to the slices of salmon.

Serve the cured salmon as a starter, a casual lunch (letting people cut their own) or as part of a buffet. Leftovers make fabulous sandwiches and canapés. It will keep for a good week, wrapped in clingfilm in the fridge, and it freezes well.

Serves 8

1 side of fresh salmon, boned, weighing around 1kg/2lb

3 tablespoons sea salt

3 tablespoons light brown sugar

2 tablespoons grated horseradish (fresh, ideally, or from a jar) or a good grinding of black pepper

2 ready-cooked beetroot (cooked without vinegar)

TO SERVE

Large tub (400g) crème fraîche mixed with a handful each of chopped mint and dill, or 2 bulbs of fennel, finely sliced and dressed with olive oil and salt

Rinse the salmon and dry it. Lay a sheet of aluminium foil, large enough to wrap the fish completely, on a waterproof tray and place the salmon on the foil, skin side down. Mix the salt, sugar and horseradish (or black pepper) and rub all the mixture over the flesh. Slice the beetroot finely and lay over the fish. Wrap the foil tightly around it. Place a board or flat-bottomed dish on the foil parcel and weigh it down with heavy objects such as tins. Place in the fridge and leave to mature for at least 24 hours and up to four days. A puddle of deep purple liquid will form in the tray: don't worry about this.

When you're ready to eat, remove the foil and brush off the beetroot and horseradish mixture. Slice the salmon thinly and serve with rye bread and mint and dill crème fraîche, or fennel salad.

A note on curing fish

Curing fish in salt preserves it, by pulling out the moisture and making an environment that is unfriendly to bacteria. We don't need to do it now, with freezers and easily accessible shops to call on, but the fine flavour and firm texture of cured fish haven't lost their appeal – think of smoked salmon.

Horseradish

If you can get fresh horseradish root, snap it up. Resembling an ugly long parsnip, it keeps for weeks tightly wrapped in clingfilm in the fridge. Grate it with the windows open (it can make your eyes sting).

As well as using it for this recipe, it makes the best horseradish sauce available. Just mix it with crème fraîche, tasting as you go to get a heat level to suit you. It makes roast beef sandwiches. Just that. It *makes* them.

Duck

Everything but the Quack (Four Ways with Duck)

When did we become so obsessed with tenderness? Fillet steak and lamb cutlets might not require much chewing but they are dull flavoured compared with many other cuts of meat. Thankfully, these days we are more tuned in to the idea that swiping the 'prime cuts' of an animal and leaving the rest isn't just a waste, it's gastronomic foolishness. The slow cook cuts and the trimmings are often the most delicious and cooked the right way, they'll be perfectly tender too.

If 'nose to tail eating' makes you feel a bit faint – and few of us have the space or the expertise to set to with a whole pig – then a duck is a good place to start, manageable even in the smallest kitchen.

Ducks, like pigs, are enormously versatile, which makes them very good value. There are the breasts, of course, the 'fillet steak' of the bird. The legs are great for casseroling, but even better cooked slowly in their own fat to make confit, southern France-style. The leftover fat is great for roasting potatoes, or use it to make the rillettes on page 173.

Best of all though are what the French call *fritons*, or sometimes *grattons*, delectably crunchy morsels made by frying the skin slowly – think of them as duck scratchings. Fritons are great with a glass of wine before dinner or sprinkled over a salad.

These recipes require two ducks, which gives quantities to feed four people generously. You can use just one duck, but you may need to buy an extra tin of duck fat to have enough to cover the legs when making the confit. Look for free range or organic farmed birds as wild ones won't have enough fat on them.

Take 2 farmed ducks...

- First separate the parts of the ducks, slicing off the breasts and cutting off the legs.
- Remove the fat and skin from the carcass (not from the legs and breasts) and render the fat to confit the legs, and make fritons – see instructions opposite.
- Make stock with the bones and giblets (reserve the liver).
- Confit the legs.
- Cook the breasts as a special supper (see Five-Spice Duck Breasts recipe on page 32).
- Make crostini with the liver.
- All the parts of the duck can be frozen if you don't want to tackle all the recipes in the next day or two.

Sorted!

Fritons and duck fat

Strip all the skin and fat from the duck carcasses and cut it into matchbox-sized pieces. Place in a small pan with a glassful of water and cook over a very low heat for about an hour, until the shrunken pieces of skin are floating in a pan of fat. Try not to let the fat get so hot that the skin starts to sizzle; you want the fat to melt, not fry. Strain the fat, allow to cool and refrigerate for up to a month, or freeze for a year. Keep the bits of skin for fritons, (described in the introduction) delicious crisp duck scratchings (or freeze them if you aren't going to make the fritons that day).

To make the fritons, heat a heavy-bottomed frying pan. Add the duck skin and fry very gently for 30 minutes or so, stirring and turning every now and then. When the fritons are a good brown colour and crisp, drain them on kitchen paper and sprinkle with salt and black pepper. Serve warm with pre-dinner drinks or scattered over a salad. They are best eaten straight away, but you can keep them in the fridge and reheat them gently in a frying pan before eating.

Duck Confit

Duck preserved in its own fat is a tradition of the southwest of France, and is the best way to eat the legs. Once cooked up, they are meltingly tender with a delectably crisp skin. Confit is best kept for a couple of weeks before eating – but it can keep for much longer, up to 3 months, provided it has a good covering of fat over it, improving with time. I prefer to use it within a month.

Serves 4

4 duck legs

4 tablespoons coarse salt

4 teaspoons brown sugar

Generous grating of nutmeg and a grinding of black pepper

6 garlic cloves, unpeeled and bruised

Duck fat, rendered from 2 ducks

Put the duck legs in a non-metallic dish and add the salt, sugar, nutmeg and pepper, rubbing them well into the duck, both skin and flesh sides. Cover with clingfilm and refrigerate for 18–24 hours, turning the legs halfway.

Preheat the oven to 130°C/gas mark 1, or make ready an electric slow cooker.

Melt the fat in a heavy-based ovenproof casserole that is just big enough to accommodate the duck, or in the slow cooker. Rinse the duck legs, pat dry on kitchen paper and slide them into the hot fat along with the garlic. Arrange the legs so that they are completely submerged in the fat, weighing down the meat with a heatproof plate if necessary. Bring to a gentle simmer and put the casserole in the oven. Cook for about 2 hours, until the meat is butter-soft – test it with a skewer. (If you are using a slow cooker, cook the legs, submerged in the fat, for 7 hours or overnight.) Allow to cool, still covered in the fat (transfer everything first to another dish or large lidded jar if it's convenient) and store, covered, in the fridge.

To cook, heat the dish gently to liquify the fat (or, if the confit is in a jar, put the sealed jar in a pan of hot water). Lift out the duck legs carefully: the meat will be almost falling from the bone. Cook skin side down in a hot frying pan until the skin is crispy, then finish off with 10 minutes in a hot oven to heat through. Eat with mash or potatoes fried in the duck fat, and a frisée salad.

Duck Pho-style

I travelled to Hanoi a couple of years ago with Stephen and Jules Wall, who own a chain of *pho* restaurants. We ate *pho*, the Vietnamese meat-and-noodle broth, at least four times a day for a week, stopping at dingy roadside stalls and hole-in-the-wall restaurants, picking up recommendations from locals and crossing town on a tip off, all in search of the ultimate *pho*.

There was only one *pho* we ate (or drank) that I thought might have been bolstered with bouillon powder, and that was at 3am in an all-night café (the Vietnamese equivalent of an after-pub kebab joint). The rest, every one, was made with a good, slow-cooked stock. Which is exactly what you have here.

Add any scraps of leftover cooked duck (and, for an authentically Asian – and delicious – touch, pop in the heart too, sliced first). If you have no leftovers, add a thinly sliced duck breast to the simmering stock, where it will cook in seconds, and serve straight away. Once you have filled the bowls with steaming broth and slippery noodles, the real fun starts. Let your guests pile on herbs, squeeze over lime juice and sprinkle with chilli sauce, until their bowls are packed with goodies.

Serves 4

1.2 litres duck stock

1–2 shallots, unpeeled

Thumb-sized piece of fresh ginger, unpeeled

100g noodles (flat rice noodles are the best choice)

Few dried shiitake mushrooms (optional)

Leftover scraps of duck

Skim the fat from the stock.

Spear the shallots and ginger on skewers and hold them in the flame of a gas cooker or char them on a hot griddle until blackened. Rinse off the loose black bits and put them in a pan with the stock along with the onions. Simmer for 30 minutes, uncovered if you feel the duck flavour needs concentrating, otherwise cover the pan.

Cook the noodles in boiling water according to the packet instructions.

Add the meat to the stock and heat through. Put a pile of noodles in each bowl and top up with stock and meat, leaving the shallots and ginger in the pan.

Serve steaming hot with the *pho* platter and a small bowl of rice vinegar with a few slivers of sliced garlic in it.

Pho Platter

1 bunch of spring onions, white parts shredded lengthways, dark green parts cut into rings

Leaves from 1 small bunch of mint and 1 small bunch of coriander

3 kaffir lime leaves, finely shredded, or a little grated lime zest

Nuoc mam (Vietnamese fish sauce) if possible, which is less salty than the Thai version *nam pla*

2–3 fresh red chillies, thinly sliced

2 limes, quartered

Duck Liver and Caramelised Onion Bruschetta

Just a little something to nibble on before supper, a crisp piece of toast with soft liver and sweet caramelised onion, a combination that reminds me of trips to Venice for Calves' Liver *alla Veneziana*.

Finely slice a couple of large onions. Heat a little olive oil in a frying pan, add the onions and a pinch of salt, cover and cook until the onions are soft. Remove the lid and continue cooking until the onions are melting and caramelised – add a little sugar or honey to help things along if you like. Stir in the leaves from a couple of sprigs of thyme and a splash of sherry, cook for a moment longer, then put to one side.

Toast a few slices of ciabatta, rub with garlic and drizzle with olive oil. Keep warm.

Take one or two duck livers and check them carefully, cutting off any green bits or membranes. Cut the liver into olive-sized chunks. Heat a little oil in a frying pan and sauté the liver until lightly browned but still pink inside. Sprinkle with a little salt.

Taste the onions and season with salt and pepper. Pile onto the bruschetta and top with the liver. Scatter with a few more thyme leaves and serve.

Five-Spice Duck Breasts

The breasts are the 'best' bit of the duck, what the fillet steak is to beef. In truth, I don't like the breasts any better than other parts of the bird, but they are easy to cook and a crowd-pleasing dish for a dinner party, especially with this vaguely Oriental-flavoured glaze. While it's traditional to serve one duck breast per person, I find that the meat is so rich that, once neatly sliced, four breasts will satisfy six people.

Serves 6

4 duck breasts

3 tablespoons runny honey

2 tablespoons soy sauce

½ teaspoon Chinese five spice

Mix the honey, soy and five spice and smear half of it generously over the duck skin. Leave for 30 minutes at room temperature and then repeat with the rest of the mixture.

Preheat the oven to 230°C/gas mark 8. Put the duck breasts skin side up on a rack over a roasting tin and cook for 10 minutes. Remove from the oven and allow to rest for at least 5 minutes. Slice and arrange on warm plates. Serve with beetroot or sweet potato mash and watercress, or spring greens stir-fried with soy and ginger.

Lemon, Lemongrass and Lime

Citrus fruits bring glamour to the kitchen all year round, but it's during chill weather that I am most grateful for them. They are at their best now, their skins still full of fragrant oil and their flesh juicy. Apart from ordinary lemon and lime, look out for their relatives. My mother, when she lived in California, used to collect Meyer lemons from her tree. They were yellow skinned, but with orange-coloured, mandarin-scented flesh that was a little less sharp than ordinary lemons. If you're lucky enough to find them, use them for a sorbet or to make an exotic lemonade.

In Vietnam, I was entranced by *kalamansi*. These look like miniature limes, but with orange flesh and a particularly fruity tang. We squeezed them over fish or mixed them with fish sauce to make an addictively sour-salt dipping sauce.

Lemongrass is not, of course, part of the citrus family, but an Asian species of grass that grows in clusters, long, coarse blades exploding out exuberantly like those mounds of pampas grass in the garden. The flavour is a gentle lemon zesty, resinous, leafy one, that can be replaced with a strip each of lemon and lime zest, although it won't be quite the same. The central, tender heart is the part that is used. Cut off all but the bottom 10cm and strip away the tough outer leaves. Finely chop the inside, which will include soft leaves and stem. The trimmings can be infused in stock to give it an Asian flavour.

Lemon Aid

- Lemon juice freezes well. When using the juice in recipes, assume 1 medium lemon yields 3–4 tablespoons juice.

- Spare lemon peel? Freeze it whole or grate the zest and mix with sugar and store in an airtight jar for up to a month. Use for lemon biscuits and cakes.

- Even the zested, squeezed-out lemon halves can be used. Dip the cut sides in salt and rub over your copper pans to scour them back to brightness.

- Store unwaxed lemons in the fridge. Waxed lemons are fine in the fruit bowl but need washing well in hot water before the zest can be used.

- If you find lemon with leaves attached, snap them up. Wash the leaves and use them as a sort of citric bay leaf, or a Mediterranean version of Asian kaffir lime leaves. Scrunch them into curries or tuck them into the belly of a fish before baking.

Vietnamese-style Chicken with Lemongrass and Caramel

Sweet, salty and fragrant, this is sticky and delicious. It's best made with inexpensive chicken thighs, which have enough collagen to cope with the long cooking, rather than expensive breast which would just dry out.

Serves 4

8 chicken thighs

4 tablespoons sugar

1 tablespoon vegetable oil

1 red onion, sliced

1 fat garlic clove, chopped

2 lemongrass stalks, peeled and finely chopped

1 teaspoon grated fresh ginger

1 red chilli, chopped

3 tablespoons fish sauce (*nuoc mam* or *nam pla*)

Strip the skin from the chicken thighs and discard. Slice away the flesh from the bones and cut into 2–3cm chunks. Set aside.

Put the sugar and 4 tablespoons water in a saucepan (one with a stainless steel or white enamel interior is best, so you can see the colour of the caramel easily). Heat gently until the sugar has dissolved, then simmer until a deep conker brown – as soon as it starts to darken, watch carefully to see it doesn't burn. Remove the pan from the heat and quickly tip in 60ml water. Stand back: it will hiss and splutter.

Heat the oil in a large pan and fry the onion until soft. Add the garlic, lemongrass and ginger, and cook for a further minute. Stir in the chicken pieces, fish sauce and 250ml water. Bring to a gentle simmer and cook for about 40 minutes uncovered, stirring occasionally, until the chicken is tender and coloured conker brown. It should be bathed in plenty of sticky brown sauce: top up with more water if necessary.

Serve with boiled rice and steamed bok choi sprinkled with sesame oil.

Mango, Chilli and Lime Salsa

A classic combination, with a vaguely Southeast Asian flavour that makes me think it was first conceived in Australia, the home of fusion food. But wherever it came from, it's so wonderful it bears repetition. Great with barbecues or Mexican food, this salsa is good with fish, especially mackerel. Grill or steam fillets or whole fish (oily fish needs to be cooked through) and spoon over the salsa. Serve with a green salad and bread or rice.

Serves 2–4

1 mango, peeled and diced

½ red onion, finely chopped

½ red chilli, finely chopped

Juice of 1 lime

Small bunch of coriander, leaves only, roughly chopped

Mix all the ingredients and leave to stand for a few minutes, or up to 3 hours in the fridge. Serve with grilled or steamed fish.

Lemon and Polenta Cake

The most famous version of this cake is from London's River Café, and very good it is. Mine is smaller, so more suitable for anyone with less than a whole restaurant to feed, a little less crumbly, to make it easier to eat with your fingers, and more lemony, because you can't have too much of a good thing. Polenta is ground-up maize, and comes graded from fine to coarse. Fine or medium is the kind to choose here, either the 'easy cook' sort or ordinary polenta.

Makes 8 slices

110g unsalted butter,
    softened

225g caster sugar

200g ground almonds

3 large eggs

Zest of 4 lemons and the
    juice of 1

110g polenta

1 teaspoon baking powder

Pinch of salt

Preheat oven to 160°C/gas mark 3. Line a 20cm round cake tin with baking parchment.

Put all the ingredients in a food processor and whizz to a smooth batter. Spoon into the lined tin and bake for 45–50 minutes, until a skewer pushed into the centre of the cake comes out clean with no uncooked batter on it. Cool in the tin.

Lemon Syrup

For an extra squidgy, lemony cake, add tangy syrup over the top:

Juice of 2 lemons
100g caster sugar

When the cake goes in the oven, mix the syrup ingredients and leave to one side. The sugar won't dissolve completely, which is as it should be. The remaining crystals will form a sugary crust on the top of the cake.

When you take the cake out of the oven, spike the surface with a skewer or cocktail stick. Spoon over the syrup and leave the cake to cool in the tin.

Tip

Leftover zested lemons won't keep for more than a day or two so squeeze out the juice and freeze it ready for lemonade and sorbets.

Lime and Coconut Rice Pudding with Mango

In Thailand, translucent, glutinous sticky rice is often cooked with coconut milk. For a softer, more familiar version, my take on the authentic dish uses ordinary pudding rice but with a gorgeous rich tang from the coconut and lime combination. Good after an Oriental-inspired main course like the Five-Spice Duck Breasts on page 32.

Serves 4

65g pudding rice

400ml can coconut milk

60g white sugar (granulated or caster)

1 vanilla pod

2 ripe medium mangoes, peeled and sliced

Zest of 1 lime (preferably removed with a zester)

Preheat the oven to 150°C/gas mark 2.

Put the rice, coconut milk and sugar in an ovenproof dish, and stir together. Add the vanilla pod.

Cover with a lid or with foil and bake for 1¼ hours. Remove the dish from the oven, give it a quick stir, and leave to cool, still covered. Refrigerate once it is at room temperature.

Serve the cold rice pudding in bowls with a few slices of mango and sprinkled with lime zest.

Lemon Barley Water

Homemade lemon barley water is refreshing but go easy with the lemon juice, since too much will spoil the gentle flavour as well as destroying the all-important mildly alkaline quality.

Makes about 1.2 litres once diluted

100g pearl barley

2 lemons

3 tablespoons sugar (or more, to taste)

Put the pearl barley in a bowl and pour over a kettleful of boiling water to scald it. Stir well, then drain.

Remove the zest from the lemons using a vegetable peeler and put it in a pan with the drained barley and 600ml water. Bring to the bowl, cover and simmer for 30 minutes.

Leave to cool, then strain the liquid into a jug. Add a squeeze of lemon juice and the sugar (save the rest of the lemon juice for another recipe). Serve diluted with iced water.

Tip

I save the lemony cooked pearl barley for a barley pilaff, mixing it with the scraps and gravy left over from a roast chicken. Tip half a sliced Savoy cabbage into the pan too, and cook until the pilaff is hot through and the cabbage is just done. Lovely for lunch.

Spring Baking

Baking is supremely satisfying at any time of the year but in Spring, turning up the oven and whipping up some treats is positively therapeutic, banishing chill and cossetting in one.

Vanilla Scones

These scones are a little rough around the edges, but keeping the dough so soft it's impossible to knead makes them the lightest ever. Delicious with blackcurrant jam and lashings of cream.

Makes 9

225g self-raising flour, plus extra for dusting

2 tablespoons caster sugar

Pinch of salt

60g butter, chilled

140ml milk

2 teaspoons vanilla extract or paste

Beaten egg, to glaze

Preheat the oven to 200°C/gas mark 6. Line a baking tray with baking parchment.

Mix the flour, sugar and a pinch of salt in a bowl. Cut the butter into pea-sized cubes and rub it into the flour until the mixture resembles fresh breadcrumbs.

Mix the milk with the vanilla extract or paste. Pour into the bowl with the flour and mix to a sticky dough with a spoon.

Dust the work surface liberally with flour. Scrape the dough out on to it. Dust more flour on top. With your hands, pat the dough into a square about 2.5cm thick.

Using a floured knife, cut the dough into nine squares like a noughts-and-crosses grid, dipping the knife in flour after every cut. Lift the squares on to the prepared baking sheet and bake for 15 minutes until golden.

Cool on a rack and eat the same day if possible.

Squidgy Apple Cake

My first kitchen job was in a pub in Wiltshire. It was no gastropub. I twisted orange slices for the salad garnish, grated boiled eggs for egg mayonnaise sandwiches, and cleaned out the fryer in which the roast potatoes were cooked every Sunday. But much of the food was good, all homemade by Karen, a Wiltshire lady in her forties with a shaved head and a ring through her tummy button, who dreamed of retiring to Cyprus to run a tea shop.

Karen broke every rule I'd learned in cookery school when she made cakes. Often she had to stop halfway through folding in egg whites, to microwave a frozen trout or heat up sticky toffee pudding. The oven was stuck permanently on the highest setting, but Karen just shrugged and baked her cakes in *bains maries*. The landlady kept us short of ingredients, so Karen improvised, golden syrup instead of honey, small eggs instead of large (although always butter, never margarine). Despite all this, her cakes turned out perfectly every time.

Karen gave me this recipe when I left, and I love it, sweet, squidgy and gently spiced. It improves if you keep it a day or two before eating. Serve cold for tea or warm as a pudding, with cream.

110g butter

225g light muscovado sugar

2 eggs, whisked

225g plain flour (wholemeal if you like)

2 teaspoons baking powder

2 teaspoons freshly grated nutmeg

2 large cooking apples, peeled, cored and diced

2 tablespoons demerara sugar

2 tablespoons runny honey

Preheat the oven to 170°C/gas mark 3. Grease a 20cm round cake tin (or a smaller tin for a squidgier result).

Cream the butter and dark brown sugar and whisk in the beaten eggs little by little. Sift over the flour, baking powder and nutmeg. Fold together, then gently mix in the apple. Pour into the prepared cake tin and bake for about an hour, until risen and browned.

Mix the honey and demerara sugar and spread over the cake while still warm. Leave to cool in the tin.

Olive Oil Madeleines

Poor old Madeleines, weighed down by the millstone of literary association. Set a plateful on the table and someone is bound to bring up *Remembrance of Things Past* and look very pleased with themselves. (A quick Google will bring you up to speed if you want to play 'top that quote'.)

Well, I can't promise that these little cakes will send you into the same ecstasies of nostalgia as Proust, but they aren't remotely dry or highbrow either. Delightfully light, with their faintly crisp outer shell, they're lovely with a cup of tea or even with ice cream or poached fruit. Olive oil adds an interesting savoury-sweetness, but if you prefer, use the traditional melted butter instead, or some nut oil if nuttiness suits.

Best of all, unlike Proust's 12-volume masterwork, you can complete these in less than 30 minutes if you have a tabletop mixer. Just set the egg and sugar beating while you prepare the rest, using tablespoon measures rather than scales to make the process even faster. The pretty scallop shell moulds can be bought from cookshops, but bun or muffin tins do as well. Either way, make these on the day you intend to eat them; these are fancies of the easy-come, easy-go variety – they don't improve with hanging around.

Makes 12–14

1 large egg

50g caster sugar (4 level 15ml spoons)

50g self-raising white flour (6 level 15ml spoons)

3 tablespoons olive oil, plus extra for oiling

A little orange zest or a few drops of vanilla extract or rosewater

Icing sugar, for dusting

Preheat the oven to 190°C/gas mark 5. Oil 14 madeleine moulds or bun tins with olive oil.

Whisk the egg and sugar until the mixture is very thick and mousse-like, and the beaters leave a clear trail.

Sift the flour on to the egg mixture and fold in gently. Then fold in the oil and orange zest or flavouring.

Put about 1 tablespoon mixture in each Madeleine shell (if you use the same spoon you measured the oil with, the mixture will slide off easily) and bake for 10 minutes, until golden. Turn out onto a cooling rack. Dust with icing sugar when cool, and serve.

Red Onion and Thyme Focaccia

Foccacia, rich in olive oil, has a very soft dough that is hard for amateur bakers to knead by hand, so use a tabletop mixer fitted with a dough hook if you have one. Giving the dough just the one rise makes the texture more open, but don't rush it by putting it in an airing cupboard or other warm place. Room temperature is plenty hot enough, and gives a better flavour.

Serves 6–8

450g strong white flour

1 teaspoon salt

1 x 7g sachet easy-blend yeast

100ml olive oil, plus extra for oiling

Leaves from 5–6 thyme sprigs

4 small red onions, each peeled and cut into 8 wedges

Sea salt flakes

Mix the flour, salt and yeast in large mixing bowl, ideally one belonging to a tabletop mixer. Add half the oil and 300ml warm water, plus the thyme leaves.

Mix with a spoon to a very soft dough, then knead with the dough hook for 3 minutes. (If you knead by hand, it will take at least 10 minutes. The dough will seem impossibly soft, but persevere, and use a dough scraper to bring the sticky mass together. Eventually it will become smooth and cogent.)

Oil a baking tin measuring 30 × 18cm and spread the dough out in the tin, squidging it down evenly. Cover with a tea towel and leave to rise for 1½ hours until doubled in size. Meanwhile preheat the oven to 200°C/gas mark 6.

Press into the pillowy dough with your fingertips to make dimples all over. Toss the onions in 1 tablespoon of oil, and drizzle the rest over the foccacia, letting it run into the dimples. Arrange the onions over the top. Sprinkle with the salt flakes.

Bake for 25 minutes, until golden and cooked through. Cool in the tin, covered with a tea towel (this keeps it soft).

Late Spring/ Early Summer

The end of spring, just as the blossom falls and the fruit begins to set, feels rich and fertile. The greengrocers, however, call it 'the hungry month', the time when the last of the stored produce is finished but the new crop is not yet ready. Even the homegrown cabbages are over.

Cooks need to hold their nerve. The courgettes are in flower and will soon be the epicure's preferred size, finger length, the strawberries are nearly there, and in a week or two the greengrocer will be stacked with local lettuces.

In the meantime, there are tender stems of asparagus and the first pink radishes. A little later the first peas and broad beans make their appearance. (Until they do, frozen peas are a good stand in, although bear in mind that their sweetness, relative to fresh peas, may change the balance of a recipe.) Keep and eye out for peashoots too, the first delicate fronds of the pea plant, and excellent in salads.

Don't forget, too, that there are other young leaves to be gathered, on country walks or even on city wasteland. Young nettles make a good soup, and it's free too, which goes some way to taking the sting out of spring.

Peas and Broad Beans

The thing about broad beans … is that the skin of the beans is tough and tannic, giving them a worthy taste. The solution, which converts them into a true delicacy, is to peel each bean.

Just pod the beans and cook them in boiling water until tender. Drain and cool under the cold tap. To peel, slit the skin with your thumbnail and squeeze out the emerald kernel within. It sounds impossibly fiddly, and it takes time, but popping the bean out of each leathery eau-de-nil capsule is curiously satisfying, like bursting bubble wrap.

True, a carrier bag full of unpodded beans yields barely a teacupful of bright green slivers, but they are sweet and earthy, without the bitterness of the whole beans. A delight.

Peas, on the other hand, certainly don't need peeling. It is often said that frozen peas are better than fresh, as they are frozen within a couple of hours of picking, before the sugars have had a chance to convert to carbohydrate. Frozen peas are remarkably sweet, and not in the least starchy. Fresh peas are variable, and also counter-intuitively more expensive, even though there is all that podding still to be done. (The reason for the inflated price is that pods have to be picked by hand while peas for freezing can be harvested by a huge machine called a pea viner, which strips and pods in a single action.)

Yet still I buy fresh peas, partly because I enjoy their lack of homogeneity, partly because in season, eating frozen seems wrong. There are some dishes, like soup, that can be too sweet made with frozen peas. But mostly, I bring home carrier bags full of pods with delicate curling tendrils still attached because I enjoy the podding, find it meditative even. It's a good job to give guests who want to help, the sort of thing that is fun to do with a friend and a glass of wine, nibbling the odd raw, fresh, firm green pea.

Flat mangetouts and tubby sugar snaps are good if you can get them really fresh. Where I live they are all airfreighted in, and taste dull and tired, especially the ready-trimmed ones with their browned tips. If you can buy homegrown, or grow your own, lucky you. They can be used to make a leafy-tasting version of the pea soup on page 52, though they are perhaps best just steamed and dressed in melted butter, sea salt and a sprinkling of poppyseeds.

Recently I've found pea shoots in the shops, either growing in punnets like cress or in a cellophane pillow pack. The tender top leaves of a young pea plant, they are good in salads, with a distinct pea flavour and a juicy crunch from the stem. And with their delicate curling tendrils, they're enchantingly pretty to boot.

Pea Shoots and Broad Beans with Orange Dressing and Air-dried Ham

Use whichever ham you like for this. Proscuitto di Parma or Serrano, Iberico or, better still, one that is local to you. It is also excellent with cooked ham, cut straight off the bone. When it comes to the vegetables, some fresh peas or asparagus tips would be lovely here, too. Just use whatever is fresh and green.

Serves 4 as a starter

A double handful of pea shoots (see page 48)

150g or ½ cupful of peeled broad beans

4–8 slices of air–dried ham

Malden or other crystalline sea salt

Leaves from a few sprigs of chervil (or a mixture of parsley and tarragon)

FOR THE DRESSING

100ml single cream

Juice and zest of ½ orange

Juice and zest of ½ lemon

sea salt

Toss the pea shoots and beans (no need to cook them) together with a fat pinch of sea salt. Arrange on a big platter, or separate plates, with the ham. Mix the cream, orange and lemon zest, then 2 tablespoons of the orange juice. Season with salt and a squeeze of lemon juice. Trickle the dressing over the salad and scatter with the herbs.

How much do I need?

Broad beans

1kg beans in the pod = about 500g shelled beans = 300g (a cupful) peeled beans

Peas

1kg peas in the pod = about 400g podded peas (less if they are very young)

Pea and Parsley Soup

Frozen peas can make a soup that is unpleasantly sweet, but balanced with the ferric flavour of parsley they work well here. Serve it in small quantities, since it can be filling. If you prefer, like me, to give people their first course before sitting down at table, then sip the soup out of teacups with pre-dinner drinks. Make the soup up to two days ahead, and if you want to really vamp it up for an at-table first course, top each serving with a freshly fried scallop.

Serves 8 as a starter

2 tablespoons butter

1 small leek, sliced and washed (discard the dark green leaves)

2 celery sticks, chopped

450g frozen peas (petits pois are a bit too sweet for this)

20g parsley leaves, chopped

300ml light chicken or vegetable stock

4 tablespoons half-fat crème fraîche

Melt the butter in a medium saucepan and add the leek and celery. Cook until the leek is soft but not coloured.

Stir in the peas, then add the parsley and stock. Bring to the boil, cover and simmer for 5 minutes.

Add 300ml cold water and transfer everything to a blender or food-processor and whizz to produce a smooth green soup. Sieve the soup back into the rinsed-out pan, using a ladle to push as much of the pea purée through as possible.

Heat gently (don't let it boil) and stir in the crème fraîche. Taste and season with salt. Blitz with a hand blender, if you have one, until the soup has a cappuccino-like froth on top. Pour into eight teacups or little bowls.

Nettle Soup

Stinging nettles make a good soup, so arm yourself with rubber gloves, scissors and a carrier bag and head for the undergrowth. Pick the smallest nettles you can find and reject any that have dangling strings, which are the plant's flowers. Cooking the nettles neutralises the sting, but puréeing a few raw leaves in a soup at the end leaves just enough to make the tongue tingle pleasantly. Leave that bit out if it worries you.

Serves 4

A carrier bag full of young nettles

2 tablespoons butter

2 small leeks, thinly sliced

2 garlic cloves, chopped

1 litre chicken stock

250ml cream

Salt and black pepper

Lemon juice (optional)

Still wearing your gloves, pull the leaves from the stems and wash well. Melt the butter in a large pan and add the leek. Cook until soft, than add the garlic and cook for another 2 minutes, without letting it colour.

Add the stock and bring to the boil. Add all but a handful of the leaves and simmer for 30 seconds. Add the cream and the rest of the nettle leaves and put in a blender or food-processor and whizz until smooth.

Rub through a sieve into the rinsed-out pan for a really smooth finish. Taste and season with salt and pepper, plus perhaps a squeeze of lemon juice.

Broad Beans, Peas and Ricotta with Grilled Spring Onions

The smoky flavour of grilled food goes well with sweet things – think of barbecue sauce and ketchup. Here it's the peas and broad beans pointing up griddled spring onions, with mild, cool ricotta as a foil. Later in the season you could replace the onions with sliced courgettes.

Serves 4 as a starter, 2 as a lunch dish

250g podded and peeled broad beans

250g shelled fresh peas

6 slender spring onions

1 tablespoon olive oil

Handful of rocket

¼ lemon

4–5 tablespoons ricotta cheese

Basil sprigs

Salt and freshly ground black pepper

Drop the beans and peas into a pan of boiling water and simmer for a minute or two. Drain and refresh in a bowl of iced water, then drain again.

Cut the spring onions into finger lengths, trimming off any coarse green leaves. Put them in a bowl with the olive oil and a pinch of salt and toss until well coated. Heat the grill or a ridged griddle until very hot. Cook the onions until browned on both sides, then return to the bowl to cool.

To serve, mix the rocket, peas and beans in with the onions. Squeeze over a few drops of lemon juice. Taste the mix and check the balance is right, adding salt, pepper or more lemon juice if necessary. Arrange on a large plate, or four small ones, and dot with teaspoonfuls of ricotta and the basil leaves. Eat straight away.

Tip

If you have any ricotta left over, mix it with a little sugar and a few drops of vanilla essence to eat with fruit.

More things to do with peas and broad beans

Spring Mix – cook peas, broad beans and baby carrots separately in boiling salted water until just done. Drain and plunge in iced water. When cold, mix together. To serve, heat a good dollop of butter in the same cooking water until bubbling, then add the vegetables and season. Stir until heated through.

Mushy Peas – not the classic marrowfat version, but still good with sausages and fish. Cook frozen peas in boiling water, drain and add a dollop of butter. Purée with a hand blender, leaving a slightly rough texture. Taste and add seasoning.

Lettuce and Pea Salad – put a cupful of frozen peas in a bowl and pour over boiling water. Leave for 2 minutes, then drain and add to a bowl of mixed salad leaves, including a few bitter ones like chicory and radicchio. Add a finely sliced spring onion and dress with vinaigrette.

Asparagus

There is something miraculous about a field of asparagus in the spring, the stiff green shoots emerging ramrod straight, direct from the bare soil. It reminds me of the story of Cadmus, and how he planted a ploughed field with dragon's teeth, whence sprang warriors armed with spears.

Asparagus has an exalted status as one of the few vegetables we consider worth eating alone, with just a buttery sauce. It's how I eat the first few bundles of the season. But as the brief season goes on, it is worth expanding the repertoire a little to add glamour to salads and tarts.

Not that anything goes. Sometimes it appears as a side dish, along with carrots, say, or buttered peas. But asparagus is a prima donna among vegetables and does not take well to anything except a starring role, upsetting the balance and upstaging the main dish.

Choose asparagus with tightly closed tips, no little buds bursting through the pointed scales, and certainly no slimy patches. Check the base, which should be dry but not wizened. And eat asparagus the day you buy it – it doesn't keep well.

To cook it, snap off the base of the stem if it seems woody, otherwise just trim the base. Very fat spears may need the bottom half peeled with a vegetable peeler, but it's not usually necessary for stems no thicker than your thumb.

If you have a tall asparagus steamer, cook the spears in that (it's great for cooking purple sprouting broccoli too). Otherwise steam the stems in an ordinary steamer, or boil them in a frying pan full of water, taking care not to overcook them or the tips will disintegrate.

Asparagus and Chicken Salad with Lemon Dressing

A quick lunchtime salad made luxurious with asparagus. Add fresh herbs to the mix – flat-leaf parsley, chives, basil, dill or chervil – if you have them to hand. Bread and a glass of rosé wine are all you need to go with this.

Serves 2–3

1 bunch of asparagus, woody parts trimmed

½ roast chicken

1 small bunch of rocket

1 cos lettuce, leaves torn into small pieces

FOR THE DRESSING

Grated zest of 1 lemon, and 2 tablespoons juice

2 teaspoons Dijon mustard

Pinch of salt

2 tablespoons olive oil

2 tablespoons single cream

Cut the asparagus into short lengths and steam until just cooked. Cool in a bowl of iced water, then drain and dry, squeezing them gently in a clean tea towel.

Make the dressing by mixing the lemon zest, juice and mustard with a large pinch of salt. Whisk in the oil and cream, then taste and adjust the seasoning, adding a little more oil if it is too sharp.

Pull the chicken meat from the bones and cut or tear it into bite-sized pieces. Mix with the rocket leaves, lettuce and asparagus. Trickle over the dressing and serve.

Other ways with asparagus

Asparagus and poached egg

Sidestep the traditional hollandaise sauce and slip a poached egg on to a pile of hot asparagus. If you can find duck eggs, so much the better.

Asparagus with Parmesan crumbs

Up to 2 hours ahead, steam or boil 500g asparagus until just done, then plunge into a bowl of iced water until cold and drain. Mix 6 tablespoons fresh breadcrumbs with 3 tablespoons grated Parmesan, 1 tablespoon chopped parsley and seasoning. Arrange the asparagus in a heatproof dish and sprinkle over the crumbs. Trickle with melted butter and grill until golden and hot through. Serves 4 as a starter.

Asparagus and orange butter

Asparagus with a blood orange-flavoured hollandaise called sauce Maltaise is a classic. I rarely feel the inclination for serious sauce making, but the combination is too good to pass up. Melt unsalted butter and season with a squeeze of orange juice (a blood orange if you can get one) and a little grated zest. Add salt and pepper and serve with steamed asparagus.

Herbs

Fresh herbs are one of the highlights of cooking, their pure taste and flavour brighten dishes immeasurably. Herbs are a year-round pleasure, but in spring they are particularly welcome, as the home crop becomes available. Even the perennial 'hard' herbs like thyme and rosemary are better in spring, their tender new shoots tasting greener and less pungent than the coarser, drier overwintering leaves. Bunches of herbs are prettiest kept in vases on the kitchen table, mixed with a few spring flowers. But, prosaically, they last longest washed, dried and wrapped in a sheet of damp kitchen roll, then put in a sealed plastic bag in the salad drawer of the fridge.

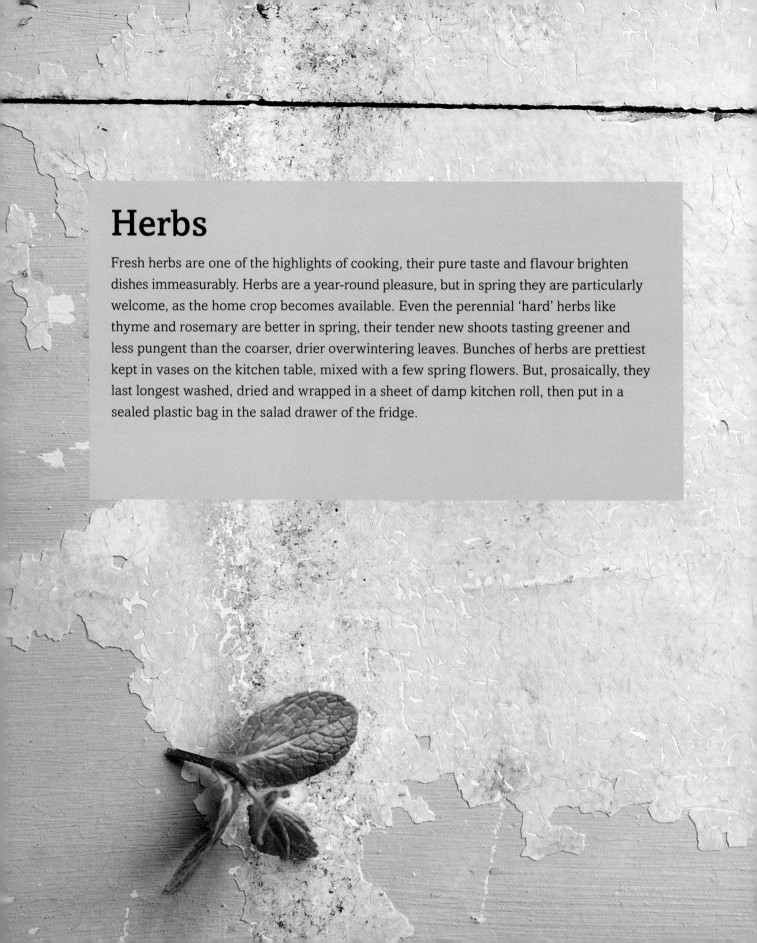

Four Fast Herby Pasta Dishes

These four recipes all use 225g pasta and are enough for two hungry people. Double the quantities for a family of four, using your biggest pan.

- Cook a tin of anchovies in 2 tablespoons olive oil until melted. Add a crushed garlic clove and a small bunch flat-leaf parsley, chopped, then stir in freshly cooked fusilli.
- Sizzle 500g cherry tomatoes, halved, in 4 tablespoons olive oil until just beginning to soften. Add a crushed garlic clove, salt and pepper and freshly cooked conchiglione. Tear over fresh basil leaves and eat with grated Parmesan.
- Fry 1 tablespoon fennel seed in 2 tablespoons olive oil until fragrant. If the oil from the sardine tin is good quality (taste it and see) then use that. Add a tin of sardines, drained, mashing them up in the hot oil. Stir in freshly cooked penne and chopped parsley or dill.
- Chop 2 ripe tomatoes and cook in 3 tablespoons olive oil until warmed through. Mix in freshly cooked penne, then stir in a big handful of fresh rocket and a pinch of sea salt. Eat before the rocket wilts with shavings of Parmesan.

Mackerel with Gremolata

Mackerel is the best of the oily fish, mild-flavoured and succulent. Pair it with gremolata, a brightly flavoured, faintly crunchy mix of parsley, garlic and lemon zest – it's delicious sprinkled over any fish but especially oily fish, cutting through the richness with a cleansing astringency. Try it with herring and sardines as well as mackerel.

Serves 4

2 lemons

2 small bunches flat-leaf
parsley, leaves only

1 tablespoon chopped garlic

4 medium mackerel, gutted

Sea salt

Preheat the grill.

Cut 12 thin slices from one of the lemons, and cut each slice in half. With a vegetable peeler, take the zest off the other lemon, and chop it finely. (Save the rest of the lemon for another dish.) Chop the parsley, and mix it with the lemon zest, garlic and a pinch of sea salt.

Wash the mackerel thoroughly and slash through the skin and some flesh of each one 3 times on both sides of the fish. Tuck half a lemon slice in each gash, and sprinkle the fish with salt.

Grill the fish for about 10 minutes on each side, until it's cooked through and the lemon slices are tinged with brown. Serve scattered with the gremolata.

A note on gremolata

Gremolata is traditionally served with osso buco, veal shin casserole, but it is good on many meat dishes – anything that needs a fresh note. Make it with orange zest instead of lemon, to sprinkle on braised oxtail or a dark beef stew.

Poulet à l'Estragon

Possibly the best chicken recipe in the world, certainly one that's stood the test of time. The faint aniseed flavour of tarragon, like star anise with beef and fennel seed with fish, intensifies the flavour of the poultry, making it both fresh tasting and intensely savoury. But beware: if you grow your own tarragon, it may be mild Russian tarragon rather than the true French tarragon, in which case you'll need to add three or four times as much. The gorgeous juices are on the thin side, so you could thicken them with a little *beurre manié* (equal parts of soft butter and flour mashed together) but I prefer to leave them as they are, and serve it in deep dishes (soup plates).

Serves 4

1 tablespoon olive oil

4 chicken leg portions

10 x 15cm sprigs of French tarragon (or, at a pinch 1 tablespoon freeze-dried tarragon, see page 59)

250ml white wine

3 tablespoons crème fraîche

Preheat the oven to 200°C/gas mark 6.

Heat the oil in a large frying pan and fry the chicken until browned on both sides. Transfer the pieces to an ovenproof dish (one that will accommodate them in a single layer).

Tip the fat out of the frying pan and pour in the wine. Bring to the boil, stirring well to release all the brown bits from the base of the pan. Pour over the chicken, and tuck in 4 of the tarragon sprigs. Transfer the dish to the oven and cook uncovered for 30 minutes. Remove the chicken from the dish and keep warm.

Tip the juices into a small pan, and spoon off the fat from the top if there seems to be a lot. Bring the juices to simmering point. Stir in the crème fraîche and the rest of the tarragon. Taste and adjust the seasoning and pour over the chicken.

Serve with new potatoes and beans or the Tomato and Courgette Gratin on page 82.

A note on dried herbs

In general, I find dried herbs vile, in particular the 'soft' herbs like parsley, dill, basil and mint. But I'll make an exception for tarragon, which keeps something of its pungency when dried. If there is no fresh tarragon then a tablespoonful of papery flakes from a jar, added before the chicken goes in the oven, will suffice. Even the classic dried 'herbes de Provence' can taste dusty unless they are excellent quality. I do keep a jar of freeze-dried tarragon. The papery flakes keep something of their pungency, as long as they are cooked, as in the recipe on page 62.

Mint and Dill Crème Fraîche

This is a gorgeous summery combination, useful for all sorts of things, and like all my favourite food, requires zilch effort to make. It's not so much that I'm lazy (although I am), more that it's supremely satisfying when three ingredients marry so well. It's what good food is all about.

Enough for 6 people with poached or smoked salmon

Bunch of dill (about 30g)

Small bunch of mint (about 15g)

Small tub (200ml) crème fraîche

Chop the mint and dill, discarding large stalks. Mix with the crème fraîche.

How to use it

- Thinned with a little water and dolloped on cold chicken
- Spooned alongside a poached salmon, with a puy lentil salad
- Mixed with 500g freshly boiled small new potatoes, to make a salad.
- With smoked salmon and rye bread

Salsa Verde

This brightly flavoured sauce, with a tang from the capers, savouriness and salt from the anchovies, sweetness from the garlic and bitterness from the mustard, really socks it to the tastebuds. My favourite condiment of all time.

Serves 4–6

1 garlic clove

4 tinned anchovies

About 10g (half a supermarket packet) each of basil and mint

About 20g flat-leaf parsley

1 tablespoon Dijon mustard

1 tablespoon capers in vinegar, drained and roughly chopped

1 tablespoon coriander seed, lightly crushed

Olive oil

Crush the garlic and anchovies together in a pestle and mortar. Discard any coarse stalks from the herbs and chop them, not too finely, in a food-processor if you like. Mix the herbs with the mustard, garlic, anchovies, capers and coriander. Stir in enough oil to make a pouring consistency.

How to use it

- Sear tuna briefly, then slice very thinly and arrange on a plate. Drizzle the sauce over the fish with Jackson Pollock aplomb.

- Eat alongside the Onglet on page 128.

- Gorgeous with baked sea bass: rub a whole sea bass with salt and olive oil, cook in a very hot oven until the skin is bronzed, and the flesh is just beginning to flake.

- Serve a bowl with roast lamb instead of harsh, vinegary mint sauce.

Herb Olive Oil

It makes sense to use a little food-processor or a stick blender to make this rich green unguent, although you could pound the leaves and garlic in a pestle and mortar instead, adding the oil gradually. It will take a while, ten minutes of hard graft at least, but your reward for stiff arms will be a gentler, sweeter flavour than the mechanically-made stuff. The oil will keep a week or so in the fridge.

Bunch of parsley or basil (about 20g) or a mixture

6 tablespoons olive oil

1 small garlic clove

Whizz all the ingredients together to a green purée in a mini food-processor.

Rosemary, Polenta and Olive Oil Biscuits

These crisp and fragrant biscuits are easy to make and delicious with ice cream or with raspberries and cream. Oh, I know, it is sacrilege to mix olive oil and dairy in one course, but there you are. They take well to other flavourings too. Try a teaspoonful of lavender flowers, the grated zest of lemon and orange, a teaspoonful of crushed fennel seed, or ½ teaspoonful of ground cardamom seeds.

Makes 8–12

150g flour

30g fine polenta

60g caster sugar

Pinch of salt

Leaves from 3 x 10cm
rosemary sprigs

90ml light olive oil
(not extra virgin)

Mix the dry ingredients in a bowl. Chop the leaves of the rosemary finely, then stir them with the oil into the mixture. Pat into a round about 0.5cm thick on a baking tray (no need to grease it, although a sheet of greaseproof paper is a good idea, as much to protect the biscuits from over-heating as anything), or use a 20cm round loose-bottomed cake tin. Mark into squares or segments with a knife. Chill for an hour in the fridge, then bake for about 40 minutes at 150°C/gas mark 2 until very lightly coloured. Leave for five minutes or so on the tray (or in the tin) then lift on to a rack to finish cooling.

Fragrant Food

With the cold weather relaxing its grip and the blossom in full bloom, now is when fragrant food seems particularly welcome. Or perhaps it's just that I've shaken off my winter cold. Either way, lavender, muscatel and rosewater, not to mention gorgeously perfumed geranium leaves, all seem to belong together, so I present them to you here.

Simple Rosewater Cake

This easy cake with its slightly crunchy glaze is lovely by itself for tea, or with summer fruits for pudding. Taste your rosewater before you start: if very strong, the result is unpleasant rather than just perfumed; the Star Kay brand, for example, is more of an essence and so you will need far less. I taste the cake mixture as I add the rosewater, stopping when it is pleasantly rosy. But then I need very little excuse to eat raw cake mixture.

Makes 12 slices

170g butter

170g caster sugar

3 eggs

225g self-raising flour

About 6 tablespoons rosewater

225g icing sugar, sifted

1 tablespoon lemon juice

Preheat the oven to 180°C/gas mark 4. Grease and line the base of a 20 × 25cm cake tin.

Cream the butter and sugar until pale, then whisk in the eggs one by one. Fold in the flour, then 4 tablespoons rosewater. Turn into the tin, spread evenly and bake for 35–40 minutes. Leave in the tin while you make the glaze.

Mix the icing sugar, remaining rosewater and lemon juice. Prick the still warm cake all over with a fork and pour over the glaze. Remove from the tin when cold and cut into squares or fingers.

Tip

Rosewater from a Middle Eastern shop is often the best, but whatever you do, don't use rosewater from the chemist. It usually has bitter compounds added to make it inedible.

Moscatel Granita

Granita is a grainy, soft-textured sorbet, exquisitely refreshing on a hot day. Properly made, it should be stirred every 8 minutes while it is freezing, but the addition of a slug of alcohol, here in the shape of sweet moscatel wine, stops the mixture from freezing solid, and makes it possible to stir it up at the last minute. Serve in chilled glasses, by itself or with sliced strawberries and a dollop of natural yogurt. Take the glasses straight to the table since the granita melts quickly.

Serves 6–8

150ml moscatel wine

850ml muscat grape juice (fresh if you can, otherwise Carmel® brand from kosher shops or the kosher section in the supermarket)

Juice of 1 lemon (or ½ lemon and ½ lime)

Mix all the ingredients and freeze in a large plastic box, one that leaves enough room for stirring, for at least 2 hours.

About 30 minutes before you intend to serve the granita, put some glasses in the freezer to chill.

Just before serving, stir the granita into a grainy slush, breaking down any large crystals with a fork or a potato masher.

Rosewater Syrup for Melon and Summer Fruit

This syrup scents a fruit salad beautifully; use it for just about any summer fruit. Watermelon with rosewater syrup and a squeeze of fresh lime is good, but melon, peaches and strawberries respond best of all.

150g granulated sugar

150ml water

1–3 tablespoons rosewater

Heat the sugar and water gently until dissolved, then boil for 5 minutes. Allow to cool. Add the rosewater gradually, tasting as you go, since they vary in strength. Use straight away.

New Season Lamb with Lavender and Crème Fraîche

Stroll through a market in Spain or Italy, and you may spot impossibly tiny legs of lamb at the butcher's counter, scarcely the size of a turkey drumstick. These are true milk-fed lamb, traditionally a spring delicacy. It has the palest, tenderest flesh, and needs careful cooking. Generally, when roasting meat I would aim for the brownest, crispest exterior possible, to maximise the delicious caramel-savoury flavours, but on spring lamb that would smother the delicate taste of the pale flesh.

If I can't get true spring lamb, and I rarely can, I still make this recipe when the first of the new season lamb appears. The lavender-scented cream is somehow right for the time of year, and very good with the meat. The first peas, or some braised lettuce are the right vegetables to eat with it. New potatoes too, of course – try to find some that are freshly dug, or at least no more than a day or two out of the ground.

Serves 4

1 whole leg of spring lamb,
  weighing about 1–1.5kg

Olive oil

1 teaspoon lavender flowers

75ml white wine

8 tablespoons crème fraîche

Preheat the oven to 180°C/gas mark 4 and put 4 deep plates to warm.

Rub the lamb with olive oil then place the leg in a roasting tin just large enough to hold the joint, and pour in enough water to come to a depth of about 1cm. Sprinkle a pinch or two of the lavender over the lamb and the water.

Roast for about 45–60 minutes, until a meat thermometer reads 63°C when inserted into the thickest part of the joint.

Take the lamb out of the tin and put in a serving dish. Set aside to rest, covering it to keep warm.

Put the roasting tin on the hob and add the wine. Spoon off the excess fat (use a gravy separater if you have one). Add the lavender to the remaining liquid and heat until it boils. Stirring all the time over a medium heat, let it reduce down to about half a cupful.

Add the crème fraîche and stir well until amalgamated. Add any juices that collect under the lamb. Taste and adjust the seasoning, bubbling the liquid down if it is too thin and copious. (The sauce will always be on the thin side. If you prefer a really thick, spoon-coating consistency, then mix 1 teaspoon cornflour with 1 tablespoon cold water, and add to the sauce, stirring until it thickens.)

Carve the lamb on to the warmed plates and spoon over a little sauce.

Tip

As with all flowers, buy dried lavender that has been grown for cooking, or use some you have grown yourself and know to be unsprayed.

Geranium-scented Coeur à la Crème

These faintly sweet cream cheeses from France are traditionally made in heart-shaped moulds, which are pretty but expensive. It's just as delicious made as one large heart in a sieve instead. Flavour the cream with a bayleaf, orangeflower water, or just vanilla, if you can't get scented geranium leaves.

Serves 6

4 large scented, unsprayed geranium (pelargonium) leaves – rose or mimosa-scented

140ml whipping cream

250g ricotta

200ml crème fraîche

50g caster sugar

2 large or 3 medium egg whites

Muslin

TO SERVE

250g dried apricots, simmered in water until soft, or 500g fresh berries or other soft fruit

Put the geranium leaves and whipping cream in a small pan and heat gently until just below boiling point. Cover and leave to infuse.

Once cool, remove the leaves and beat the whipping cream, ricotta, crème fraîche and sugar together with a wooden spoon. In a separate bowl, whisk the egg whites to soft peaks and fold gently into the cream mixture. Line 6 *coeur à la crème* moulds or a sieve with a double layer of muslin, allowing the extra to hang over the sides. Fill the moulds or sieve with the cream mixture, folding the muslin overhang back over the top. Place on a tray deep enough to accommodate the whey that will drain out of the cream as it sets. Refrigerate for 1–3 days: the longer you leave it, the firmer it will be.

To serve, unwrap the top of the moulds or sieve. Turn out onto a plate and peel off the muslin. (If you have used a sieve, then gently shape the cream into a heart shape before removing the muslin.)

Prettying it up

While it is traditional, and admittedly delicious, to drench this dessert with more pouring cream, I prefer to make a coulis by puréeing and sieving about half the apricots or soft fruit. Sweeten it lightly (it may need a squeeze of lemon juice, too, especially strawberries) and drizzle over the *coeurs à la crème*. Decorate with more fruit scattered around and serve.

High Summer

Summer days call for easy food that doesn't require standing over a hot cooker, low-fuss dishes that can be eaten outside if the weather allows. This is the time to eat food in and from the garden. That doesn't have to mean your own garden. Of course, that's the ideal, and the coolest – these days serving your own homegrown veg is as hip as trickling balsamic vinegar over polenta in the 90s. But the tender, ultra-fresh produce from farmers' markets is a very good alternative.

The best ingredients are those that only appear in their true season, rather than being air-freighted in from the other side of the world. Right now, look for the fruits, such as cherries, strawberries, peaches and melon, as well as the 'vegetable fruits', such as courgettes and aubergines.

It's all about time and place, like the rough local wine that tastes divine on holiday, and goes with the traditional local dishes brilliantly. Take it home and it just won't be the same. In the same way, however good it is, a strawberry in winter has lost its joy.

Maybe it is the high water content of those cool-flavoured foods such as watermelon and cucumber that make them as good on a hot day as ice lollies and granitas. But even in a chilly summer, winter warmers like steamed puddings would be odd. So perhaps the extra daylight primes us for the juicy, the tangy and the fresh.

Aubergines

Tight-skinned, polished ebony, with their voluptuously pendulous shape, the only aubergines available in my early days as a cook were sexy and exotic enough. Now there are many more to choose from, including almost spherical violet ones that are particularly fleshy and good for slicing and grilling, and small oval white ones that are the root of the American name 'egg plant'.

Old cookery books advise slicing and salting aubergines, to draw out their bitter juices. Modern varieties, like those shiny, midnight purple ones, don't need this treatment, but I still do it with more unusual kinds, which may still be acrid. Dust the pieces with salt (about a teaspoonful for each large aubergine), pile them in a colander and leave in the sink for an hour or so. Rinse well and dry before using.

Aubergine's mild, buff–coloured flesh is a natural partner for olive oil, soaking it up in the frying pan like a thirsty sponge. If this worries you, keep on frying, and it will release some oil back into the pan. Drain the cooked pieces through a sieve to lose as much as possible before incorporating in a dish.

Ways with aubergine

Griddled Aubergine with Mint and Goats' Cheese or Feta

Cut the aubergine into 1–2cm slices. Brush with olive oil. Heat a griddle to very hot and cook the aubergine on each side until striped with brown and cooked through. Arrange on a plate and dot with a scattering of crumbled cheese. Tear mint leaves over and drizzle with olive oil. Put lemon quarters on the side to squeeze over.

Roast Aubergine and Peppers with Harissa

Toss chunks of aubergine and red pepper in olive oil mixed with a little harissa (see page 86) in a roasting tin. Roast for 40 minutes at 200°C/gas mark 6, stirring once or twice during cooking. Serve with Greek yogurt and couscous, plus extra harissa.

Caponata

Soft and slippery, with a complex sweet-savoury-sour flavour, caponata is a sassy Sicilian answer to ratatouille. It keeps beautifully for two or three days so make double, and eat it with grilled meat or fish the first night, then with salads for lunch the day after, then pile the last spoonfuls on bruschetta to serve with drinks the following day.

I nearly left this recipe out of the book for being too long, but in the end I couldn't help myself. It's just so delicious, and after all, most of the ingredients can be picked up on a trip to the greengrocer or market, and the others are probably already in your cupboard.

Serves 4

125ml olive oil

1 large aubergine or a few small ones, trimmed and cut into cubes

1 large onion, sliced

1 fat garlic clove, chopped

2 peppers, deseeded and cut into matchbox-size pieces

1 fennel bulb (save the frondy tops) or 6 celery sticks, sliced

2–3 large, very ripe tomatoes

½ glass of red wine

Juice of ½ lemon or 2 tablespoons red wine vinegar

1 teaspoon sugar

Handful of green olives, pitted

2 tablespoons capers

Basil leaves (optional)

Salt and freshly ground black pepper

Heat enough oil to generously cover the base of a large frying pan.

First cook the aubergine in batches until lightly browned and soft, adding more oil if necessary. Scoop out into a sieve suspended over bowl. Repeat with the onion, garlic and peppers, and finally the fennel or celery. Reuse the oil that collects in the bowl as you go, using fresh oil to supplement it.

Put the tomatoes in a bowl and pour boiling water over them. Count to ten, then drain them and run under cold water. Peel off the skins, then squeeze the tomatoes so the seeds squirt out into the bowl. Chop the tomato flesh roughly.

Put the wine and lemon juice or vinegar in the pan with the sugar and bring to the boil. Add the tomatoes and cook until the mixture has reduced to a thick sauce. Season with salt and pepper, stir in the cooked vegetables and leave to cool to room temperature.

Before serving, mix in the olives, capers and the basil or the frondy tops of fennel. Taste and adjust the seasoning, adding more salt, sugar, lemon juice, olive oil or pepper if it needs it.

Aubergine Pizza

This is far from authentic, and would probably appal a Neapolitan, but never mind: it's delicious. Because it isn't laden with cheese that can go rubbery, it is great to serve at room temperature as well as hot. Eat it with a glass of red wine as a lazy supper. It's good cold too so take the leftovers on a picnic or put them in a lunch box.

When you roll the dough (or pastry, for that matter), stop about 2cm from each edge, so the edges stay a bit thicker. If you 'roll off' the edges with the pin they become so thin they burn. If you're making only one pizza, roll out the second half on a sheet of baking parchment. Lay on a baking tray and freeze. Once firm, lift of the baking tray and wrap well, then return to the freezer. Use straight from frozen.

Serves 4

300g prepared pizza dough
  (see below)

500ml tomato passata

1 medium aubergine

Olive oil

1 bunch spring onions,
  thinly sliced

Flour, for dusting

50g goats' cheese

Salt

Preheat the oven to 250°C/gas mark 8 or as high as it will go. Have ready a large sheet of non-stick parchment or a pizza tray with holes in it that allows steam to escape so the base gets really crisp. If you are going the paper route, then put a large baking tray in the oven to get hot.

Put the passata in a small pan and simmer until it is thick as Greek yogurt. Leave to cool.

Slice the aubergine as thick as a coin and drizzle with olive oil. Mix the spring onions in a bowl with 3 tablespoons olive oil.

Roll and stretch the dough out on a lightly floured surface to a circle about 35cm across. Lay it on the paper or pizza tray. Spread the tomato sauce to within a couple of centimetres of the edge. Arrange the aubergine slices, overlapping, on top. Crumble over the goats' cheese and sprinkle with salt.

Transfer to the oven on to the hot baking tray (unless using a pizza tray) and bake for 10-15 minutes until the aubergine is starting to brown. Remove from the oven and spread the onions and olive oil on top. Transfer the pizza directly onto the oven shelf. Turn the heat down to 200°C/gas mark 6 and bake for a further 10 minutes or until touched with gold.

Pizza Dough

Enough for
2 x 35cm pizzas

450g strong white bread
  flour

1½ teaspoons easy-blend
  yeast

1 teaspoon olive oil

Pinch of salt and a pinch
  of sugar

Put all the ingredients in a bowl with 250ml warm water. Mix to a soft dough (adding a little more water if it feels stiff) and knead for 10 minutes, pummelling it until it is smooth and stretchy. (If you have a table-top mixer with a dough hook, 45 seconds with that will be enough.)

Put the dough in a bowl and cover with clingfilm. Leave to rise at room temperature for 1½ hours until doubled in size, then knead again for a few seconds. Unless you intend to use the dough straight away, just give it a very brief knead every hour or so to return it to its original size.

Courgettes

It is a truth universally acknowledged by gardeners that wherever courgettes are grown, there are too many, and they are too big. The problem would be easily solved by picking them when they are smaller, less watery and with a finer flavour. That way we eat more and better courgettes. But somehow the urge to let them swell to baby marrows, watery and tasteless, is irresistible.

In fact, a good courgette is no more than 15cm long. It should be hard, with a shiny skin. Occasionally in markets in France and Italy I've seen finger-sized courgettes, which are gorgeous cooked whole in butter. These infant courgettes often have their canary yellow flowers attached, which, if they are very fresh, can be stuffed and steamed. Use a little ricotta, flavoured with herbs and garlic, to fill them, twisting the tops to seal the little bundle. Then the flowers can be dipped in flour and deep-fried ideally, but if not, fry in a frying pan with about 1cm of vegetable oil. Eat with a little tomato sauce.

After a few hours the petals tend to stick to each other, making it impossible to open them out for stuffing, but they are still good shredded and added to an omelette or a salad, where they lend a mildly peppery kick.

Ways with courgettes

Huge courgettes tend to be watery and disappointing. For these recipes stick to ones about 15–20cm long. If you can get smaller ones, so much the better – but you'll need a few more.

- Slice 3 courgettes lengthways, 0.5cm thick, and rub the slices with olive oil. Cook on a hot griddle until striped with dark brown, turning once. Lay the slices on a platter and scatter with just 1 tablespoon of crumbled feta and plenty of torn mint leaves. Trickle over olive oil. Serve at room temperature.

- Heat 2 tablespoons of butter until sizzling and add 1 teaspoon crushed fennel seed (give them a quick bash in a pestle and mortar first to release their aroma) and ½ chopped red chilli. Slice 3 courgettes lengthways, 0.5cm thick, and fry until patched with brown. Grate over the zest of ½ lemon and season with salt and pepper. Eat with fish or lamb.

- Slice 3 courgettes diagonally, about as thick as a pencil. Dip them in a saucerful of flour, then a beaten egg and finally into 4 tablespoons breadcrumbs or polenta mixed with 2 tablespoons grated Parmesan and lots of black pepper. Heat enough vegetable oil to fill a frying pan 1cm deep. Drop the slices straight into the hot oil and cook, turning once, until golden. Eat hot from the pan.

- Slice 4 courgettes and 250g mushrooms 0.5cm thick and cook in butter until lightly browned, then mix in a good dollop of crème fraîche, chopped mixed herbs and seasoning. Eat with grilled chicken or fish.

Tomato and Courgette Gratin

A very simple gratin with no breadcrumb topping to eat with roast lamb or just about any simply cooked meat. Cut the tomatoes and courgettes in rounds a little thicker than a pound coin, and keep them in a single layer so that they don't go soggy.

Serves 2

Olive oil

3 small courgettes, sliced

1 garlic clove, crushed

A few thyme leaves or oregano sprigs

6 plum tomatoes, sliced

Salt

Preheat the oven to 190°C/gas mark 5. Oil a large ovenproof dish, or 4 small dishes (those individual terracotta tapas dishes are ideal) generously.

Sprinkle the courgettes with salt and leave for at least 10 minutes. Pat dry. In a bowl, mix the courgettes with 1 tablespoon of olive oil, the garlic and thyme or oregano.

Arrange the tomatoes and courgettes in the dish or dishes, as overlapping slices in tight concentric circles, bearing in mind that they will shrink when they cook. Drizzle over a little more oil and cook for about 20 minutes until browned.

Pasta, Courgettes and Pine Nuts

Shaving courgettes with a potato peeler is a great trick to make delicate, professional-looking ribbons. They are pretty served raw in salads, or will cook in seconds without going soggy. In this dish, the courgettes mimic the pasta, giving the dish a lighter texture. I love young summer thyme shoots, which are milder flavoured than mature thyme, but you could use basil, chervil or parsley instead.

Serves 2

170g good-quality tagliatelle (the Cipriani brand is expensive but worth it)

3 courgettes

2 tablespoons olive oil

4 tablespoons pine nuts

1 garlic clove, crushed

A few sprigs of young thyme, leaves only

3 tablespoons freshly grated Parmesan

Salt and freshly ground black pepper

Cook the tagliatelle according to the packet instructions. Meanwhile, use a potato peeler to shave the courgettes into ribbons.

Heat the olive oil in a large pan, and add the pine nuts. Cook until golden brown, then stir in the courgettes, garlic and thyme.

Mix in the drained pasta and Parmesan. Taste and season with salt and pepper if it needs it. Eat straight away.

Chillies

Chillies are as indispensable as peppercorns in the kitchen. To pepper's dried-spice, fragrant heat, chillies riposte with a fruity, sweet fire. The hardest thing to determine is how hot a chilli is going to be. The truth is, you can't know. Judging the heat of chillies without tasting is a mug's game. While some chilli varieties tend to be hotter than others, the heat of each individual chilli can vary, even between two from the same bush.

There is nothing for it. You have to taste each chilli before adding it to a dish. Cut it in half and take a tiny slice from the stem end including a little of the inner white rib. This is the hottest part of all, not, as is often said, the seeds. Eat your sliver, and assess the heat.

And while I'm on cutting, the best advice is to use rubber gloves when cutting chillies, especially if you suspect them to be hot, to stop the capsaicinoids (the chemicals that cause the heat in chillies) from burning your skin. Wearing gloves is a pain (I worry about slicing the glove) but I am usually sorry if I haven't bothered.

The different varieties of chilli are numerous. Chilli-lovers can become quite nerdy on the subject, but with a few exceptions I don't think it is worth worrying unduly about identifying all of them.

Look out for:

- *Piment d'espelette* – a speciality of the Basque region of France, generally sold dried, these large dark red chillies have a smoky sweet flavour and a mild-to-medium heat.

- **Bird's eye** – slender, pointed red or green chillies around 4cm long. Very hot, good in Thai dishes or sliced in spicy broths.

- **Scotch bonnet** – dumpy, irregularly shaped chillies, usually red or yellow, about 4cm across. Very hot, with a citrus flavour, and good in West Indian curries. The Habañero is closely related.

- **Jalepeño** – a mild to medium green chilli (more wrinkled ones tend to be hotter) that is good in Mexican cooking.

Dried Chillies

It took a trip to Malaysia for me to really understand about dried chillies. It wasn't the only thing I learned. In temperatures of 40°C beneath the swirling fans of a Malacca hotel, Malaysia's answer to Keith Floyd showed us how to prepare banana flower, pick the best shrimp paste and mix a Nonya curry. But most importantly, he let us taste a myriad of different chillies, and we realised how drying a chilli gives it a completely different flavour, a sweet caramelised heat rather than the capsicum-scented kick of a fresh chilli.

It is dried chillies you need to make the spicy North African condiment harissa. I buy fairly mild fresh chillies when they are cheap and thread them on cotton using a needle, then let them dry in the kitchen. Ready-dried ones are just as good, although tend to be hotter. Up to you.

A note on dried chilli in the spice rack

Dried ground chillies are called cayenne or cayenne pepper, whereas chilli (or chili) powder is a blend of spices, including some cayenne. Chilli flakes are, thankfully, exactly what they say – flakes of whole dried chillies.

Rose Harissa

Homemade harissa makes a great fridge standby, and is far cheaper than buying one of the good varieties. You could tart things up with other spices (a little ground cumin is good) but I like it simple so that the chilli flavour, not just its heat, sings through. If your harissa is too hot, bearing in mind you'll be eating it by the smear rather than the spoonful, then add a grilled chopped red pepper (skinned and deseeded) to the mix, pounding it in well.

3 large dried red chillies
1 garlic clove
1 tablespoon rose water
Olive oil
Salt

Soak the chillies in boiling water for 30 minutes until soft. Drain and chop finely (scrape out the seeds and inner membrane first if you want to make a milder version).

In a pestle and mortar, crush the garlic with a pinch of salt to a purée. Mix in the chopped chillies and pound the mixture again. Stir in the rose water and then the olive oil, mixing vigorously.

Store the harissa in a jar in the fridge, where it will keep for a week, or longer if you coat the surface with a film of olive oil.

Ways to use harissa

- Add spice and a subtle fragrance to casseroles
- Mix into salad dressings for extra kick
- Spread thinly on bruschetta and top with crème fraîche or thick yogurt and a few coriander leaves
- Make rouille (see below)

Rouille

Rouille is the rich, spicy sauce often served with a French fish soup but is also good for many fish dishes. It can be made by simply mixing mayonnaise and puréed chillies, but I prefer the old-fashioned bread-based version.

3 red peppers, grilled, peeled and deseeded
1 slice of good bread, crusts removed
1 tablespoon rose harissa
2 tablespoons olive oil

Whizz everything in a food-processor until blended to a rough paste. Taste and add more oil or harissa to taste. Make up to a week ahead and store, covered, in the fridge.

Cherries

You can't have two bites at the cherry, someone said, presumably because a cherry is too small. These days cherries are often huge, almost the size of apricots, definitely big enough to go at twice. They don't necessarily have a better flavour though. I prefer the little ones such as the creamy-yellow and scarlet 'transparents' found in the southeast of England.

Sour cherries, such as Morello, are hard to come by but best for cooking, with their true, slightly almondy cherry flavour. On a recent trip to St Petersburg, every stall of the indoor food market seemed to sell two or three different varieties of sour cherry from Azerbaijan, Samarkand or other evocative-sounding sources. They were the finest cherries I've ever eaten, not mouth-puckeringly sharp, just tangy and refreshing. I'd eat them every day if I could.

Closer to hand, sweet cherries make an irresistible end to a meal, simply piled in a bowl where they shine darkly like garnet marbles. For cooking though, it's as well to boost the flavour with a little cherry firewater or kirsch, which you can make yourself (see page 90).

Duck and Cherry Salad

Duck and cherries is a classic combination, and this vividly coloured salad is richly flavoured and summery without being fatty. I like to use a whole roast duck but it is undeniably neater-looking if you use just duck breasts. Up to you. Either way, some boiled new potatoes added to the salad leaves will turn it into a one-dish meal.

Stoning all those cherries might seem a lot of work, but it's the sort of job you can give to a guest who wants to help. It's a very companionable task, like shelling peas, a good way to spend a few minutes together on a summer afternoon. If your guests are not amenable, then invest in a cherry-stoning gadget: they really work, and you can use them for olives too.

Since the best cooking cherry, the sour Morello, is hard to find fresh I've added a few dried sour cherries to boost the flavour of the regular variety. If you're lucky enough to have a Morello cherry tree in your garden, then replace all the cherries, dried and fresh, with Morellos.

Serves 4–6
(8 as a starter)

1 whole duck or 4 large
   duck breasts

2 teaspoons honey

500g cherries, pitted

30g dried sour cherries

100ml white wine or water

Splash of sweet chilli sauce

Salt

FOR THE SALAD

1 tablespoon balsamic vinegar

4 tablespoons olive oil

150g salad leaves

50g shelled pistachios,
   chopped

Large handful of basil leaves

Preheat the oven to 180°C/gas mark 4. Dry the skin of the duck with kitchen paper and pierce it all over with the point of a knife. Rub with salt and smear with the honey.

Roast for 45 minutes (for a whole duck) or 20 minutes (for duck breasts) then remove from the oven and leave to cool. Pour off the fat and juices into a bowl and put the bowl in the fridge.

Meanwhile, put half the fresh cherries, the sour cherries and the wine or water in a pan. Bring slowly to the boil, and simmer until the liquid is reduced to a tablespoonful or so, and is slightly syrupy. Turn off the heat, and leave, covered, to cool.

Spoon the fat off the juices in the fridge and add the juices to the pan. Liquidise the contents of the pan with a pinch of salt and a splash of chilli sauce. (A stick blender or a mini food-processer do the job well.) Stir in the remaining cherries.

Pull the skin off the duck and slice or tear the meat into manageable pieces. Duck breasts can be decorously cut into 2mm slices.

Whisk the vinegar with a fat pinch of salt, then beat in the oil. Dress the salad leaves. Scatter the duck over the leaves, trickle with the cherry sauce, and sprinkle the nuts and torn basil leaves on top.

A final note

This is an ideal recipe to make ahead, which will allow the fat to solidify on the dark juices, making it easier to remove. Chilling the sauce will thicken it a little too, as the natural gelatine in the duck juices gels. But do allow the meat to come back to room temperature before serving.

Homemade 'Kirsch'

Kirsch, not to be confused with sweet cherry brandy, is a clear *eau-de-vie* infused with cherry stones, and is one of the most useful of all cooking alcohols. A spoonful of this bitter-almond flavoured booze is fantastic not just with cherry puds but any of the plum and peach family, or sprinkled over slices of fresh pineapple. Kirsch is eye-wateringly expensive though, so I make my own, using the stones left after a family cherry feast.

You can do the same with plum stones, which are easier to extract from their shells. It makes a stronger-flavoured spirit with a similar flavour, perhaps a little less refined, but still good for cooking.

30–60g cherry stones (from about 450g cherries)

a small bottle of vodka (35–50ml)

Wash the cherry stones if you feel it's necessary. Put them in a strong plastic freezer bag and smash them using a mallet or the base of a saucepan (I find it easiest to lay them on a paving slab in the garden to do this).

Pour a quarter of the vodka into a jug.

Once all the stones are broken open, use a funnel to transfer them into the vodka bottle. (You could pick through and remove the shells first, but I don't bother.) Top up with the vodka in the jug if there is space.

Seal the bottle tightly and leave to macerate for at least a couple of months, topping up with more cherry stones as you get them. To use, strain through muslin or a tea strainer.

Ways with kirsch

- To finish a long hot lunch outdoors, or as a poolside snack, chill cherries by half filling a bowl with ice and scattering cherries over. Sprinkle with kirsch for fragrance.

- **Fresh Cherry Cake:** Beat 100g self-raising flour with 100g soft butter, 100g sugar and 2 eggs. Stir in 2 tablespoons kirsch and a handful of stoned cherries. Scrape into a lined 20cm cake tin. Bake at 180°C/gas mark 4 for about 40 minutes until golden and cooked through. Dust with icing sugar, and serve with thick cream.

- Cook a cupful of stoned cherries with 1 tablespoon of kirsch and 2 tablespoons of sugar until the fruit is soft and the juices bubbling. Taste and add a squeeze of lemon if necessary. Serve with ice cream or pancakes.

Melon

Big, heavy and fecund, melons are the most voluptuous of the summer fruits. Charentais are the best, with a creamy-green skin and pistachio green segment markings. They are sometimes called French Canteloupe, but the finest often come from Italy. Piled in the market, prices will vary enormously, but for once both buyers and sellers know what they are doing. The pricier melons will be better, with deep orange flesh that is at once honey-sweet and deeply perfumed. A good one can be smelt in the next room.

Other melons have their charms too, as long as they are fully ripe. Canteloupe, the orange-fleshed green melon with a mesh of rough light brown markings on the skin known as 'netting', is good eating, sweet and lightly perfumed. Galia, similar looking to Canteloupe but with a darker green beneath the netting, and pale green flesh, can be almost honey-sweet. Even the insipid Honeydew, a yellow rugby ball with pale flesh, is refreshing and sweet on a hot day.

Watermelon is a quite different beast, another genus in fact, *Citrullus* rather than *Cucumis*. The French give it a completely different name, *pastèque* rather than *melon*, as do the Italians (*anguria*, rather than *melone*) and the Spanish (*sandia* not *melon*). Only the Germans lump the two together as we do in English, with *Wassermelone*.

The dark green ones have the deepest pink flesh, speckled with dark seeds, but if these bother you then opt for the white and green striped 'tiger' watermelons. The flesh is a little paler, but they have only a few soft white seeds.

Choosing melon

- Once cut, melons don't keep well, so buy a whole one, rather than a portion, and eat it all.

- It's important to buy melons that were picked when the fruit was properly mature, so check it is the right colour (this won't change after picking).

- The stem falls off when the fruit is mature, so make sure that the one you pick no longer has a stem attached, which could mean it was picked too soon.

- There should be a little give at the other end when pressed if the fruit is ripe, but no soft patches. If your finger leaves a dent, reject it. Watermelon should be hard all over.

- Trust your nose. Give the fruit a good sniff: if it doesn't smell headily of melon, it won't taste melony either.

Watermelon and Feta Salad

Crisp, sweet watermelon is surprisingly good with salty feta, just as cucumber is. It looks beautiful too. Eat it as part of a summer lunch or a pretty pink-and-white first course.

1kg watermelon

Juice of ½ lime

1 tablespoon olive oil

150g feta cheese, crumbled

2 spring onions, finely sliced (green parts included)

Leaves from a small bunch of mint, roughly torn

Salt

Cut the flesh from the watermelon and finely slice. Put the strips of rosy pink watermelon into a bowl and squeeze over the lime. Trickle with olive oil, and mix in a pinch of salt, the crumbled feta, spring onions and mint leaves.

Three ways with watermelon

Crisp, sweet watermelon is gorgeous, but once cut it doesn't keep more than a couple of days in the fridge. Here are some ideas to use it up.

Watermelon Granita

Cut the flesh from a 1kg chunk of watermelon into cubes and purée in a food-processor. Rub through a sieve into a bowl (discard the seeds and any other debris left in the sieve). Stir in 2 tablespoons sugar and 3 tablespoons vodka, then pour into a wide plastic container. Cover and put in the freezer for at least 3 hours, or up to 2 days. When ready to serve, leave to soften for a few minutes: the vodka should stop it setting rock-hard anyway. Stir vigorously with a fork to break it up into a mass of ice crystals: don't do this in a food-processor, since it will be too fine: think hail, not snow. Spoon into glasses and serve straight away.

Watermelon and Blackberries

Dissolve 100g white sugar in 100ml hot water, add a vanilla pod and simmer for 2 minutes, then leave to cool. Cube the flesh of a large chunk of watermelon and mix with fresh blackberries. Add enough of the syrup to moisten.

Wedges

With the last of the watermelon, cut it into wedges and then triangular slices, rimmed on one side with the green rind. Pack in freezer bags and freeze. Eat from frozen as impromptu ice lollies.

Charentais Melon Water Ice

A voluptuously melon-scented sorbet, palest orange and gloriously refreshing on a hot day. Do use a melon that smells properly melony though, even a little fermented – for once it doesn't matter if it is a bit battered and bruised. In fact, so much the better if it is.

Serves 2–4

1 overripe Charentais melon, with a heady scent

TO FLAVOUR

Caster sugar, orange flower water, lemon juice, vodka or melon liqueur (such as Midori®)

Chilled glasses, to serve

Discard the seeds and rind of the melon and whizz the flesh to a purée using a blender. Taste and add flavourings as necessary: a really good melon won't need any although I usually can't resist splashing in a little orange flower water.

Churn in an ice-cream machine following the manufacturer's instructions. Then scrape into a plastic box and freeze.

To freeze without a machine tip into a plastic box and freeze until nearly solid. Cut up into chunks and whizz in a food-processor until smooth. Return it to the freezer, repeating the process if necessary, until the texture of the water ice is smooth. Allow to soften slightly before serving.

Summer Berries

Strawberries, raspberries, blackcurrants, redcurrants, blueberries, mulberries – these are the sweetshop of the season. They look enticing, taste even better, and they are easy to eat with no fiddly peeling or stoning. Berries are great for the cook, as they are the simplest of puddings on their own, and make fancier dishes look fabulous, just tumbled over the top.

The only caveat is that the sugar levels of the fruit vary enormously. Currants always need help in the sweetener department, but strawberries may be so sweet already that they do better with a few drops of lemon juice instead of or as well as sugar. Taste them and see.

Good, even, deep colour is what you look for in soft fruit. This is true of strawberries in particular, and when they are white around the stem they are probably dull tasting. But as with melons, the best guide is your nose. If they don't smell fantastic, the flavour, formed in great part by the same volatile compounds, is never going to be much cop.

Ricotta-Mascarpone Cream, Summer Fruit and an Orange Flower Syrup

I first ate this at the house of Caroline Yates, chef and cookery teacher, and since then have made my own version countless times. It's the best accompaniment for summer fruit. Sometimes I line a 25cm or 30cm tart case with sweet, rich homemade shortcrust pastry and bake it until it is biscuity crisp. Once cool, the cream can be piled in, tumbling the berries over dramatically (see page 149).

Serves 4–6

FOR THE SYRUP

2 tablespoons sugar

2 tablespoons honey

2 tablespoons water

1 tablespoon orange flower water

FOR THE CREAM

250g ricotta

250g mascarpone

2 tablespoons caster sugar

1 tablespoon vanilla essence (not vanilla flavouring)

juice of ½ lemon

Lots of fresh summer fruit, and perhaps a few Medjool dates

Make the syrup first. Mix the sugar, honey and water in a small pan. Heat gently until the sugar is dissolved, then bubble for a couple of minutes. Allow to cool slightly, then stir in the orange flower water – you may want to add a bit more than a tablespoonful, depending how strong it is. Leave to cool completely.

Mix the cream ingredients together, pile on a serving plate and chill.

Prepare the fruit, destoning and cutting it into chunks where necessary, then tumble it on the cream. Trickle over the syrup and serve.

To make sweet shortcrust pastry see page 149.

Raspberry Millefeuille

A huge piece of patisserie oozing vanilla cream and raspberries makes a showstopper of a pud that's impressive but surprisingly easy to make. It looks difficult to cut too, but in fact slices quite neatly using a sharp serrated knife and a gentle sawing action. A cake slice is the thing to transfer the pieces neatly.

Cooking the puff pastry pressed between two baking sheets keeps the pastry flat while still allowing it to bake evenly into 'a thousand leaves'.

Serves 6

225g sheet of ready-rolled all-butter puff pastry

1 tablespoon icing sugar

FOR THE CRÈME PÂTISSIÈRE

2 egg yolks

30g caster sugar

3 level tablespoons corn flour

2 level tablespoons plain flour

300ml milk

1 teaspoon vanilla extract

300ml double cream, lightly whipped

Raspberries

Preheat the oven to 200°C/gas mark 6.

Unroll the pastry and lay it on a baking sheet lined with a piece of baking parchment. Prick it all over with a fork. Lay another piece of baking parchment on top and a second baking sheet on top of that.

Bake in the oven for 10 minutes, then reduce the heat to 170°C/gas mark 3 and bake for a further 10 minutes, until golden. Cool the flat piece of pastry on a rack.

Once cool, trim the pastry into a neat oblong with a serrated knife. Cut the oblong into three strips.

Preheat the grill to high (or use a blow torch). Dust the icing sugar through a fine mesh sieve evenly over the pastry. Grill the pastry until the sugar has melted to a shiny glaze. Allow to cool. (This can be done up to two days ahead).

Make the crème patissière. Beat the eggs with the sugar, cornflour and flour. Add 4 tablespoons of milk and beat until smooth.

Heat the rest of the milk until boiling and pour it over the egg yolk mixture. Stir well, then pour back into the rinsed-out pan. Heat until boiling and thick, stirring all the time, then pour into a bowl to cool. Press a layer of clingfilm on the surface to prevent a skin forming. Leave to cool completely.

Layer the pastry pieces with the cream filling and raspberries and serve in slices.

Pain Perdu with Raspberries

French toast, eggy bread, Poor knights of Windsor...there are plenty of names for this custardy fried bread confection. It's really a sort of instant bread-and-butter pudding, the perfect rich sweet foil for a tumble of raspberries or blueberries, or any soft fruit.

Serves 4

3 eggs
150ml milk or single cream
1 tablespoon honey
4 x 1.5cm slices of brioche
1 tablespoon butter
Salt

250g raspberries

Whisk the eggs with a pinch of salt. Whisk in the milk or cream and honey.

Put 2 of the slices of brioche side by side in a dish in which they will only just fit snugly. Pour over the egg mixture. Prick well with a fork to ensure the liquid soaks in.

Heat a non-stick frying pan and add the butter. Once the butter is melted and bubbling, use a fish slice to transfer the soaked brioche into the pan. Put the last two slices of bread in the remaining liquid, pricking and turning so they are well soaked.

Fry the brioche over a medium heat for 2 minutes on each side. Transfer to a plate and put them in a low oven while you fry the remaining two pieces of brioche.

Serve the pain perdu with the fruit and some whipped cream if you like.

Quick Blackcurrant Jam

I love the intense flavour of blackcurrants. This quick jam has a soft set (you can cook it longer and test a few drops on a cold saucer if you prefer it firmer) but the brief cooking keeps the fresh, leafy flavour of the currants. Delicious on rice pudding or with vanilla scones on page 40.

Makes 2 x 250g jars

250g blackcurrants
250g sugar

Sterilise washed and rinsed jars by putting them upside down in the oven at 140°C/gas mark 1 for 30 minutes, or by putting the damp jars in the microwave for a minute.

Strip the blackcurrants from their stems and put them in a small pan with 110ml water. Bring to the boil and simmer until the blackcurrants are soft (no more than 5 minutes).

Remove from the heat and stir in the sugar until it has dissolved. Return to the heat and bring to the boil. When it reaches a rolling boil, that is when the entire surface is bubbling vigorously, remove from the heat.

Pour into the clean jars and leave to cool. The jam will thicken over 24 hours – if you can leave it that long. Store in the fridge and eat within a couple of months.

Raspberry and Hazelnut Cake

Rasperries with hazelnut meringue was a nineties staple, but I prefer the flavours in a moist, nubbly cake rather than chewy and too often over-sweet meringue. Eat it plain for tea or as a pud with more raspberries and cream or the crème patissière in the Raspberry Millefeuille recipe on page 99.

Serves 8

100g blanched hazelnuts

150g caster sugar

85g unsalted butter, softened

2 eggs

125g self-raising flour

170g raspberries, plus extra to serve

50g good-quality dark chocolate, melted

Preheat the oven to 180°C/gas mark 4 and line a 20cm cake tin with baking parchment.

Put the hazelnuts in a food-processor with the sugar and whizz until the nuts are chopped fairly finely. Add the butter and then the eggs to the hazelnut mixture, one at a time. Add the flour and pulse until mixed.

Spread two-thirds of the mixture into the cake tin. Scatter over the raspberries, then dollop over the last of the mixture, spreading it out. Bake for 40–50 minutes, until golden and a skewer pushed into the cake comes out clean.

Leave to cool, then trickle with chocolate. Serve with cream or crème fraîche and more raspberries.

In a nutshell

- Keep open bags of shelled or ground nuts in the fridge or freezer, as they quickly turn rancid. Nut oils and sesame oil should be kept in the fridge too, as they won't last more than a month in a kitchen cupboard.

- To skin hazelnuts, bake them in the oven at 180°C/gas mark 4 for 10–15 minutes, until a nut rubbed between your fingers sheds its skin. Tip the lot onto a tea towel, gather the corners together and rub until all the nuts are skinned.

- To skin almonds or pistachios, put them in a heatproof bowl and pour boiling water over them. When the water is cool enough to put your hand in, take out the nuts one by one and pop them out of their skins.

Strawberries with Raspberry Purée

Strawberries *are* summer, yet unless you are lucky enough to be able to buy the glorious, deep-flavoured variety Mara des Bois, they can need a little help. Raspberries are their best friend, with an acidity and vinous intensity that bolsters the strawberry flavour without overwhelming it. The strawbs look beautiful too, cloaked in crimson sauce.

Getting ahead
Make the Raspberry Purée up to 2 days ahead and store in the fridge. Prepare the strawberries up to 3 hours before, and keep the platter covered but not in the fridge. Coat with the sauce 30 minutes before serving.

Serves 4

500g strawberries

125g raspberries, fresh or frozen

Icing sugar or sugar syrup (see below)

Take a slice off the top of each strawberry, which will remove the stalk. Place, tightly together, pointed end up, on a platter. Cut any very large ones into quarters, but keep the pieces together so that they look whole, and place carefully with the others.

Purée the raspberries in a food-processor and rub through a sieve to remove the seeds. Sweeten to taste with icing sugar, or a splash of sugar syrup, which gives the purée a beautiful clear colour.

Use a large spoon to coat the mountain range of strawberries with a layer of sauce. Leave for about 30 minutes for the flavours to mingle before serving. A biscuit such as the citrus ones on page 203 or a piece of almond cake is the perfect accompaniment.

Sugar syrup

To make a sugar syrup, put 150g granulated sugar in a pan with 150ml water. Heat gently, stirring, until the sugar is dissolved, then boil for 5 minutes. Cool and store in a jar in the fridge.

Zabaglione Gelato with Mulberries

Here's a more traditional egg custard-based ice cream. If you can't get dark, sweet mulberries, then eat it with raspberries or poached peaches (see page 115), or as an *affogato*, a gorgeously Italian way to end a meal. Just put a scoop in a glass with a shot of hot espresso poured over the top and serve at once.

Serves 4–6

5 egg yolks

110g caster sugar

6 tablespoons Marsala

225ml milk

280ml double cream

Whisk together the eggs, Marsala and sugar in a heatproof bowl.

Bring the milk to boiling point and whisk into the egg mixture. Put the bowl over a pan of barely simmering water and stir until thickened – if you have a thermometer, you want to get it to about 66°C. When it's the consistency of unwhipped double cream, take the bowl off the heat and stir in the cream.

Allow to cool completely then churn in an ice-cream machine following the manufacturer's instructions. Then scrape into a plastic box and freeze. To freeze without a machine, tip into a plastic box and freeze until nearly solid. Cut up into chunks and whizz in a food-processor until smooth. Return it to the freezer, repeating the process if necessary. Allow to soften slightly before serving.

Summer Party

Summer and parties go together like Kate and Wills. There's more space when the weather's good enough to use the garden, and there are longer days to enjoy. Add to that brightly coloured clothes, and maybe even some heat-induced indolence. Whatever the reason, summer brings out the holiday spirit.

But parties do cause stress, especially the wedding anniversary or engagement party family affairs, and not all of it the culinary angst. There will be a mixture of ages, a lot of different people to keep happy and (if they are anything like my family) plenty of criticism for the cook to field.

So the menu needs to be uncontroversial without being boring, catering enough for vegetarians as well as meat eaters. And since feeding all those people can be daunting, keep it simple and go for self-service. I hate the word buffet, which brings back memories of soggy quiches, wilting salads and overcooked poached salmon, but with care they can be memorably good.

Seven top tips

- First, limit yourself to two or three really good main dishes, one of which is meat-free. Add a green salad, a starch such as rice or potatoes, and perhaps one other salad.

- Since everything will be eaten from the same plate, and probably in the same mouthful, make sure that the flavours go well together. No point making the perfect Oriental duck salad if it's going to be scoffed in the same mouthful as tomato, basil and mozzarella.

- As for puddings, something divinely rich and then a fruit salad or compote is plenty. Just make sure they go together, like tiramisu and raspberries, or caramel oranges and chocolate orange cake.

- Arranging the food is crucial. Garnishes don't last, but a green salad looks stunning next to a plate of vivid red tomatoes. And put out lots of tongs, by far the best implements for picking up food one-handed.

- Vary the height of dishes – this looks more interesting and makes food at the back easier to reach. Use cake stands, create platforms by sliding boxes underneath the tablecloth or sit large shallow bowls on huge stockpots.

- A white sheet makes the best tablecloth, since it will come right down to the ground. Pots of growing herbs, bottles of oil, pepper grinders and bowls of mixed breads make better decoration than non-edible fripperies like flowers.

- As part of the buffet, the following dishes will feed 10. When multiplying up, bear in mind the oldest rule in catering: the more people there are, the further the food goes. So, doubling the quantities will feed not 20 but 22 or 24. To serve 100, eight times the original quantities will suffice.

Menu

All these recipes serve 10, and can be multiplied up

Leek and Goats' Cheese Tart

Chicken and Mozzarella with Homemade Pesto

Salsa Verde and Seared Beef Carpaccio

Green Salad with Parmesan

Potatoes with Lemon and Mustard

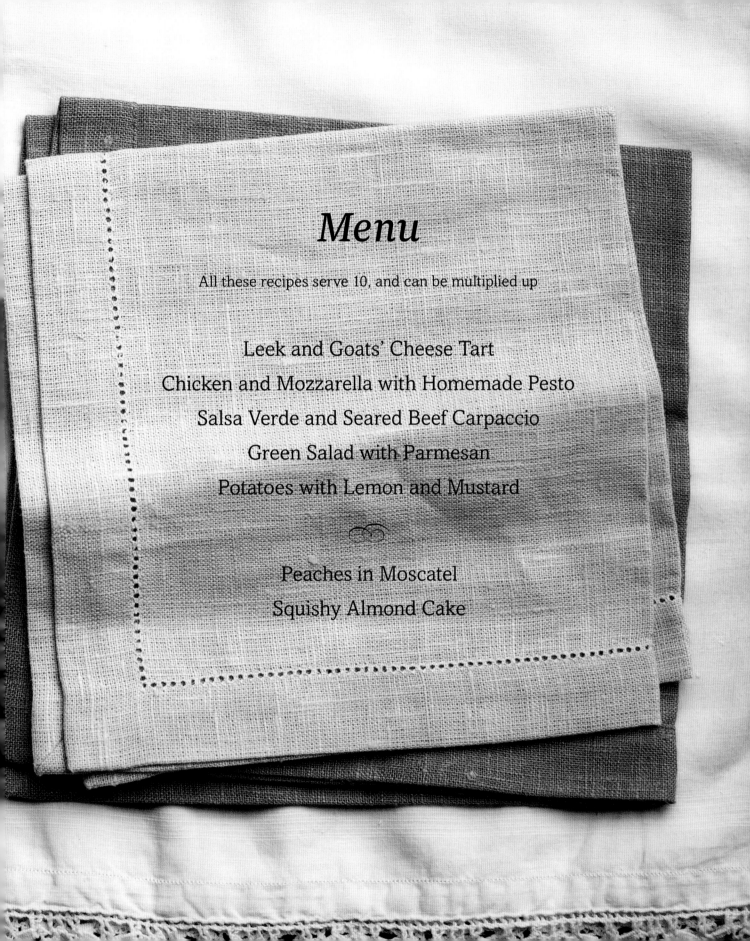

Peaches in Moscatel

Squishy Almond Cake

Seared Beef Carpaccio

I used to make this with tuna loin, in the heady days before we knew how endangered are the yellowfin, and more so the bluefin tuna fish. Should stocks ever recover, I recommend it to you. In the meantime, beef works beautifully, and is of course the 'original' carpaccio ingredient.

The story goes that the Countess Amalia Nani Mocenigo visited Harry's Bar in Venice in 1950, and announced that she was under doctor's orders to eat only raw meat. The chef covered a plate with slices of beef pounded paper thin, and drizzled over a sauce of thin mayonnaise.

The dish was named Carpaccio, after the 15th-century Venetian painter whose pictures are saturated with deep red, and who was the subject of an exhibition in the city at the time. Perhaps the vividly coloured dish caught the eye of other customers. For whatever reason, soon they all wanted some, and the dish became a menu fixture.

I sear the outside of the meat first, which gives an interesting variation in flavour and texture. It also kills any bugs that may be lurking. I don't think it is necessary to pound the meat, as long as you slice it really finely.

The delicate translucent slices are gorgeous with the punchy salsa verde (see page 65), but if you prefer, just thin a cupful of mayonnaise with milk to a pouring consistency. Season it and flavour with a little smooth mustard, grated horseradish or Worcestershire sauce, and trickle, Jackson Pollock-style, over the meat.

Getting ahead
Sear the meat up to a day in advance. Slice it up to an hour ahead, and keep the dish in the fridge, covered with clingfilm pressed on to the surface. This is one dish that is good eaten straight from the fridge, but don't add the sauce until just before serving.

Ask the butcher for a 600g piece of beef fillet taken from the middle of the fillet, so not the fattest end but not the skinny tail either. In cross section it should ideally be 5–10cm in diameter.

Serves 4–6

600g beef fillet

1 tablespoon crushed
   peppercorns

Roll the meat in crushed peppercorns until coated. Place a dry, heavy-bottomed frying pan over a high heat. When it is very hot, put the beef in and cook for a few seconds on each side, turning carefully, so that it is evenly seared all over. The idea is that the heat should have penetrated around 0.5cm in all the way round. Wrap tightly in clingfilm and leave to cool.

Slice paper thin: this is easiest if you put the wrapped meat in the freezer for an hour first. Lift each slice as you cut it onto the serving dish or board, overlapping them neatly. Drizzle over some salsa verde (recipe on page 65), and put the rest of the sauce in a bowl nearby.

Chicken and Mozzarella with Homemade Pesto

Not the cutting edge of modernist cuisine, I grant you, but the sort of food that everyone likes. Freshly made, with good ingredients, it is really worth eating. Chicken breasts aren't generally my favourite part of the bird, but they make for a neat finish to the salad, which is helpful if you are feeding a crowd that includes picky eaters (and don't they always?). Alternatively, you could use 2 whole roast chickens, meat pulled from the bone and sliced.

Getting ahead
The pesto can be made a day in advance
The chicken is best cooked on the day (chilling tends to toughen the meat a little) but could be done the day before. Store it in the fridge and let it come to room temperature before serving.
Mix the salad up to an hour before, but add the avocados as late as possible.

8 chicken breasts

Splash of white wine or vermouth

Herbs (a few thyme, oregano or parsley sprigs)

4 avocados

4 mozzarella balls

1 x quantity fresh pesto (see opposite)

50g toasted pine nuts

Small basil leaves

Preheat the oven to 180°C/gas mark 4.

Lay the chicken breasts in a roasting tin, splash in some wine or vermouth, tuck a few herbs in amongst them, cover with foil and bake for 20–25 minutes, rearranging the chicken halfway through. When they are done they should be springy, not soft or hard. Remove from the tin and allow to cool.

Dice the mozzarella into grape-size pieces, and slice the chicken and avocados. Mix in the pesto, adding a little more olive oil if necessary. Taste and season carefully. Tip into the serving bowl and sprinkle over the pine nuts and a few basil leaves.

Tip

Slicing or dicing avocados is much easier if you don't peel them. First get rid of the stone. Cut the avocado in half. Whack the sharp blade of the knife against the stone, so that it bites into it. Twist the knife slightly to remove the stone. Now with a table knife (not a super sharp chef's knife) slice through the flesh of the avocado, without cutting through the skin. Cut crossways as well if it is diced avocadoes you are after. With a large spoon, scoop out the flesh, straight into the salad.

Homemade Pesto

This pesto is miles away from the acrid, salty, dusty-tasting stuff that comes in a jar. Traditionally, it is made by pounding the ingredients using a pestle and mortar, which is well worth trying, as it makes for a sweeter-tasting pesto without that faint bitterness that machine-made versions sometimes have.

However, here we need a dressing-like pesto, smooth enough to coat the ingredients, unlike the handmade version, which tends to streakiness. A food-processor it is. Pesto is best eaten the day it is made but it will keep for 3 days in the fridge, provided it is covered with a thin layer of olive oil.

A really large bunch (about 170g) of basil

100g Pecorino or Parmesan

100g pine nuts or cashew nuts

1 garlic clove, peeled

170ml (or more) olive oil

Salt

Strip off any hard stalks from the basil and discard (I wouldn't worry about the young, soft stalks). Place the basil in a food-processor along with the cheese, nuts and garlic. Process until chopped fairly finely. If the colour is not bright green enough, add a small handful of parsley, or a few blanched spinach leaves and process again. With the motor running, dribble the oil into the pesto until it is a nice soft consistency. Taste and add a little salt if necessary.

Leek and Goats' Cheese Tart with Thyme Pastry

Leeks and goats' cheese make the most fantastic combination, the sweetness of the leeks balanced by the salty, pungent cheese. If you prefer, use long slices of Brie, arranged like the spokes of a wheel, or Cheshire cheese crumbled over.

Getting ahead

The pastry can be made up to a month in advance and frozen, then baked up to a day ahead.

The filling can be made a day ahead and kept in a covered bowl in the fridge.

The tart is best filled and baked on the day of the party but could be made a day ahead. Keep it in the fridge overnight and allow it to come back to room temperature before serving.

FOR THE PASTRY

Leaves from a large handful of fresh thyme sprigs

100g butter

200g flour

2 eggs, separated

Salt

FOR THE FILLING

4 really large, 6 medium or 8 small leeks, cut into slices 5mm thick, white and pale green parts only

60g butter

425ml double cream

6 egg yolks

200g goats' cheese log

Salt and freshly ground black pepper

Make the pastry first. Put the thyme leaves with the butter, flour and a fat pinch of salt in a food-processor and whizz until well blended. Add the egg yolks and whizz again briefly, until the mixture resembles coarse fresh breadcrumbs. Stop the machine and squeeze together some of the crumbs to check if they hold together. If not, add one of the egg whites and blend again briefly.

Tip the 'crumbs' onto a plate. Press together into a disc, cover the plate and refrigerate for about 30 minutes.

Preheat the oven to 200°C/gas mark 6. Roll out the pastry to line a 30cm loose-based flan tin, saving any scraps. Prick the base well and bake blind, covered with a sheet of baking parchment and weighed down with beans or rice, for about 15 minutes, removing the paper and beans or rice for the last few minutes. The pastry should be straw coloured and cooked through.

Use the scraps of pastry to patch up any cracks which have appeared in the pastry, and brush with the last egg white to seal it thoroughly. Return to the oven for a further 3 minutes to dry the egg white. Remove from the oven and set aside while you make the filling. Lower the oven to 180°C/gas mark 4.

Soak the slices of leek, separating out the rings a bit, for about 30 minutes in a large bowl of cold water. Scoop out, leaving any grit and dirt at the bottom of the bowl, and dry in a salad spinner or in a large tea towel.

Melt the butter in a large frying pan, add the leeks and stir until well coated with butter. Cook until soft, and all the liquid has evaporated. Allow to cool slightly.

Whisk together the cream, egg yolks, ½ teaspoon of salt and a good grinding of black pepper, and add the leeks. Tip into the prepared pastry case and distribute the leeks evenly. Slice the cheese into six or so slices. Discard the ends of rind, but I think it's fine to leave the soft, edible rind around each slice. Arrange the slices on the tart.

Bake for 30–40 minutes, until the tart is lightly browned but still slightly wobbly in the centre. Serve warm (not hot) or at room temperature.

Potatoes with Lemon and Mustard

Mayonnaise-rich potato salads are too heavy for this kind of party, or indeed any kind of party. A vinaigrette-based, lemon-spiked potato mix with a kick of mustard does the trick instead.

Getting ahead
Best made up to 4 hours ahead and kept in a cool place other than the fridge

1.3kg baby new potatoes

FOR THE DRESSING

Zest of 2 lemons, and juice of 1

1 tablespoon wholegrain
  mustard

170ml olive oil

1 teaspoon salt

Freshly ground black pepper

Fresh dill, chopped (optional)

Boil the potatoes in well-salted water then drain. If the skins are at all tough, peel them off as soon as the potatoes are cool enough to handle.

Mix the rest of the ingredients to make a dressing and pour over the warm potatoes. Serve warm or cool, but not cold from the fridge.

Green Salad with Parmesan

A simple salad, and a combination with which most people will feel familiar, and comfortable. No point in trying to be too clever.

Getting ahead
Make the dressing up to two days in advance.

300g mixed salad leaves

Small piece of Parmesan

FOR THE VINAIGRETTE

2 tablespoons balsamic vinegar

¾ teaspoon salt

Freshly ground black pepper

1 teaspoon Dijon mustard

2 teaspoons honey

8 tablespoons olive oil

Whisk together the vinegar, salt, pepper, mustard and honey. Then gradually whisk in the oil to make a thick vinaigrette.

Dress the salad leaves only as the first guests start to serve themselves from the buffet. Using a potato peeler, quickly shave ribbons of Parmesan over the salad.

Poached Peaches in Moscatel

Poached peaches, their soft shiny flesh sweetly perfumed with dessert wine, make an exquisite finale to a meal, and are easier to pull off than perfectly ripe fresh peaches.

Getting ahead
Can be made up to two days in advance and kept in the fridge.

500ml Moscatel wine (or any
  inexpensive sweet wine)

3 tablespoons white sugar

1 vanilla pod

5–6 nearly ripe peaches

Put the wine in a small pan with the sugar. Use a sharp knife to slit the vanilla pod down its length and add it to the pan. Heat the wine gently until the sugar dissolves, then bring to the boil.

Halve the peaches and remove the stones.

Slide the peaches into the pan, reduce the heat and simmer for 20–30 minutes until tender, turning occasionally if they aren't fully submerged.

Remove the peaches carefully and slip off the skins. Boil the liquid hard until reduced to a syrupy sauce. Pour over the peaches and leave to cool.

Serve with the zabaglione ice cream (page 104), and perhaps a few raspberries.

Tip
Don't waste your time trying to poach rock hard fruit for this recipe, the kind that you know won't ever ripen properly, or will be mealy textured. Instead, cook them the same way, but purée them. Use this to make Bellini cocktails, the speciality of Harry's Bar in Venice (purists will point out that it should be made with white rather than yellow peaches, but I don't think we need to be a stickler here). Just put a spoonful of the purée in the bottom of a champagne glass, half-fill with prosecco, stir, and top up with more prosecco.

Squishy Almond Cake

This is the almond equivalent of a chocolate fudge brownie. Even marzipan-haters love it: since it has no almond essence in it, the almond flavour is much less harsh. The cake is only an inch or so deep, but quite rich, so serve it cut into small slices.

Getting ahead
Make the cake up to two days in advance, and store tightly wrapped in clingfilm. Or make it a month in advance, and freeze it.

1 tablespoon each of flour and sugar, for dusting

170g butter, plus extra for greasing

170g caster sugar

4 medium eggs, lightly beaten

170g ground almonds

Icing sugar, to serve

Preheat the oven to 180°C/gas mark 4. Line a 23cm cake tin with a large sheet of foil, pressing it right into the edges and up the sides. Leave any overhang, ready to lift the cake out. Grease the foil and any exposed tin well, and dust with the tablespoonful of sugar and then the flour.

Whisk the butter and sugar together until white and fluffy. Add the eggs, a teaspoonful at a time, to the butter and sugar, whisking continuously. All this is best done in a table-top mixer. If the mixture looks as if it might curdle, add a tablespoon of ground almonds. Don't worry too much if it does curdle: the cake won't rise so well, but this isn't a disaster.

When all the egg has been incorporated, fold in the almonds, using a metal spoon or a large rubber spatula. Scrape the mixture into the tin, and spread it out very gently.

Bake for about 45 minutes, until a skewer inserted in the middle comes out clean. Check halfway through that the cake isn't browning too much: cover with a piece of greaseproof paper to prevent this.

When cooked, lift the cake out of the tin using the foil, and leave to cool, still on the foil, on a rack. Peel off the foil and dust well with icing sugar before serving.

Early Autumn

Early autumn has a glorious *fin-de-siècle* feel about it for the cook. Winter might be just around the corner, but right now there's an almost indecent bounty. We revel in peppers, aubergines and plums, and tomatoes reach their zenith in both quantity and quality. There are courgettes still, until their hard-skinned sisters, the 'winter' squashes take over. Fresh nuts too, and figs all turn up for the culinary party.

There are the first of the pears, for which I have waited all summer long, mellow and honeyed. Apples too, the sweet, tart early crop, which don't keep well but are gorgeously crisp and tangy now. And not forgetting the second round of raspberries, the autumn crop, like a last hurrah for summer, the final flourish before the serious, tough-skinned cold-weather crop starts coming in in earnest.

Unkindly, the weather always seems to get better the moment the children go back to school, and there are lunches in the garden to snatch. The ingredients are perfect for an Indian summer, Mediterranean vegetables made for a mezze to nibble on while sitting out in the last of the sunshine.

The lingering warm days are insanely precious, like the final mouthful of cake or the scrapings from the bottom of the bowl of ice cream, or the last dance at a party, more delicious because there's no more. Until next year, at least.

Figs

Figs are the most sensual of fruit, the one the ancients associated most with fertility. No wonder, when the baby-soft skin encases such a seductively moist, flame-red heart, composed not simply of seeds but of over a thousand tiny fruits. Fecundity indeed. The taste, though, is earthy, mysterious and subtle unless you can gather them sun-hot and burstingly ripe from the tree. To bring out those divinely musky flavours, look to sweet-salt combinations. Just think of that clichéd, but nonetheless fabulous starter of soft figs and tissue-paper thin Parma ham.

When it comes to puds, creaminess is good with figs, but keep it light. Ultra-rich mascarpone or even double cream has a mouth-coating quality, gorgeous in its way, but masking the fig's fragile flavour. Stick to lower fat ricotta or a mixture of Greek yogurt and cream, and add something crunchy, whether toasted nuts, thin biscuits or a glassy crisp caramel.

As for poaching, baking, jams and compotes, I'm less keen. The delicate flavour needs cosseting rather than drowning. Cooking figs is a risky (in gastronomic terms) business, too often reducing them to a sweetly bland fruit with an admittedly interesting seeded texture.

I suspect most of those cooked recipes originate in fig-rich parts of the world. In Turkey, source of the maroon-coloured Brown Turkey figs and the excellent Bursa Black, or southern Italy, home of the green Kadota, one might well need to look for ways to use up a glut of figs.

Fast Figs

- Wrap fig quarters in proscuitto and fry in olive oil, turning until the proscuitto is crisp. Eat with drinks before dinner.

- Make a salad of red chicory, sliced figs and torn parsley leaves, dressing it with olive oil, sea salt and a few drops of balsamic vinegar.

- Mix chunks of figs with raspberries, sprinkle with caster sugar and lemon juice, and leave to macerate for 1 hour. Scatter with mint leaves and serve with almond biscuits.

- Mix a tub of ricotta with a tub of mascarpone, 1 tablespoon caster sugar and 2 teaspoons vanilla essence. Pile on a plate with fig quarters, drizzle with honey and serve.

- Make a fig zabaglione by putting 4 egg yolks with 4 tablespoons caster sugar and 4 tablespoons marsala in a bowl placed over a pan of simmering water. Beat with an electric hand-held whisk for 10 minutes, to make a pale foamy mass. Cut 4–6 figs into slices and pile into four glasses. Top with the zabaglione and serve.

Pot-roast Pheasant with Beetroot and Two Kinds of Fig

The soft sweetness of figs tempers the gamey flavour of pheasant, and the unctuousness of the dried fruit makes up for the bird's tendency to dryness, while the fresh fruit relieves the richness. Pot-roasting is a good method for guinea fowl, too. All you need to serve with the dish is mashed potato (or game chips, deep-fried, thinly sliced potatoes, for traditionalists) and some fresh watercress.

Serves 4

6 slices streaky bacon

200g cooked beetroot (not in vinegar)

1 thyme sprig

150g dried baby figs

150ml (generous glass) white wine

150ml water

2 pheasants

2 fresh figs, cut into eighths, to finish

Salt and freshly ground black pepper

Preheat the oven to 160°C/gas mark 3.

Chop three of the streaky bacon slices into matchsticks, and cut the beetroot into chunks. Put the chopped bacon, beetroot, thyme and dried figs in the base of a flame-proof lidded casserole (one that can be put on the hob as well as in the oven). Pour over the wine and water.

Season the pheasants with salt and pepper and put them in the casserole, breast side down. Cover the casserole with foil or greaseproof paper and put the lid on, to make a tight seal. Roast for 1½–2 hours, until the pheasants are tender.

Turn up the temperature to 200°C/gas mark 6. Remove the lid and foil and turn the birds breast up. Cut the remaining three slices of bacon in half and lay over the breast of the pheasants. Return the casserole to the oven (uncovered) and roast for 10–15 minutes until the meat is browned.

Remove the pheasants to a serving dish and keep warm. Put the casserole on the hob and boil to reduce the juices, to make a sauce consistency. If the liquid needs thickening (it depends on whether the figs have burst or remained whole), then scoop out a few of the figs and some of the juice and purée with a hand blender before returning to the pot.

Stir in the fresh figs and warm through. Taste the sauce and adjust the seasoning.

Fennel

Florence fennel, or fennel bulb, is the thing here, not fennel seed, which comes into its own in the potato recipe on page 128. It belongs to the same family as the seed, the feathery bronze fennel and fennel herb, but has a swollen stem base, the 'bulb'. I haven't been able to discover why it is called Florence fennel. Certainly it is popular, and much cultivated in Italy, but why not Tuscan fennel or Pisa fennel? Perhaps the alliterative combination was just more memorable.

Fennel, like onions and ogres (if you believe Shrek), is constructed of layers. Each one, thick, pure white, and crisp, cups the last until they form what we refer to as the bulb. The feathery green leaves on top are a bonus, which you can use, chopped like dill, to garnish your dish, or in another dish altogether.

It is a versatile vegetable, good both cooked and raw. In salads it has a distinct aniseed flavour, but combined with a clean freshness that all but the most dedicated aniseed-phobes will enjoy. When cooked, it is transformed to a mild tenderness, juicy and with enough natural sugar to caramelise a little in a roasting pan. Added to casseroles it acts as a sort of flavour enhancer, just as fennel seed and star anise do, but its milder note makes it especially good with fish.

Preparing fennel

Chop off the frondy tops and long green stems and save for another dish. Trim the base. Examine the outer layer. If it looks a bit ropey, then pull it off (save it for the stock pot). Now you are ready to go.

Three ways with fennel

Roast Fennel with Parmesan

Cut 2 large fennel bulbs into 8 segments each, so that the layers are still joined at the bottom of each segment. Melt 3 tablespoons butter and toss the fennel in it. Arrange in a single layer in a heatproof dish and sprinkle with 3–4 tablespoons grated Parmesan. Bake for 40 minutes at 190°C/gas mark 5 until golden and tender. Serve with simply cooked meat.

Fennel and Orange Salad with Olives

Thinly slice a bulb of fennel and segment an orange using a sharp knife (see the recipe on page 204 for Oranges with Saffron). Arrange both on a plate and scatter with black olives. Sprinkle with olive oil and serve.

Bagna Cauda with Fennel

In a blender or mini food-processor combine 100ml olive oil, 50g melted butter, 8 anchovy fillets and 3 chopped garlic cloves. When smooth, heat gently in a small pan. Cut a head of fennel into sticks and dip these in the bagna cauda. Enough for 4 people as a starter.

Marinated Fennel and Chilli Salad

I first ate a salad like this at a restaurant in England owned by seafood chef Mitch Tonks. Super-simple and delicious, the fennel salad is great with any smoked fish: salmon of course, but splash out on pole-and-line caught tuna, trout or sturgeon if you feel the urge. Or serve with the home cured salmon on page 26. Whichever way, the crisp, faintly medicinal aniseedy fennel cuts through the oiliness of the fish perfectly without overwhelming the flavour.

The best tool to slice fennel is a Japanese spiral slicer, followed by a mandolin, but a sharp knife and a steady hand will do the job as well.

Serves 4–6

2–3 fennel bulbs, sliced paper thin

Zest of 1 lemon, removed with a zester

1 mild red chilli, deseeded, very finely sliced

2 tablespoons olive oil

Sea salt

Mix the fennel, lemon zest, chilli and olive oil, and scatter with sea salt crystals. Eat straight away or refrigerate for up to 2 days. Serve at room temperature.

Tip

You might expect this salad to need a squeeze of lemon juice for acidity. It doesn't. The crystals of salt and the chilli provide the bite.

Pan-fried Onglet with Fennel Seed Roast Potatoes

Onglet is sometimes nicknamed butcher's steak because, as it ages more quickly than the rest of the carcass, the butcher would cut it out before the hanging of the rest had been completed, and take it home for his tea. The cut, from the diaphragm of the cow, comprises two long pieces, each about the size of a cucumber, attached along their length with white fibre. It is very lean with a loose, almost feather-like grain, so it needs to be cooked no more than medium rare and sliced diagonally against the grain. The reward is the best, most intensely flavoured meat you can imagine. Known as hanger steak to the Americans, the English name is thick skirt, but that means it is often confused, even by butchers, for ordinary skirt steak, so I prefer the unambiguous French name, onglet.

The resting time means the steak is served warm rather than hot, but it will be deliciously tender and packed with flavour.

Serves 4–6

1 whole onglet

Oil

2 tablespoons butter

Salt and freshly ground black pepper

Heat a large frying pan to very hot. Rub the onglet with oil and season with salt and pepper.

Add a little oil to the pan and sear the steak on all sides to a good deep brown. Reduce the heat to medium and add the butter, letting it melt and sizzle. Cook the steak to rare or medium-rare (no more, or it will be tough), basting it with butter all the time.

Leave to rest on a warm plate for at least 10 minutes before slicing. Serve with any juices from the pan or resting dish poured over, and the Fennel Seed Roast Potatoes below or a bowl of salsa verde (page 65).

Fennel Seed Roast Potatoes

Serves 4–6

1kg small new potatoes

Rapeseed oil, duck fat or other roasting fat

2 tablespoons fennel seed

Small bunch of flat-leaf parsley

Salt and freshly ground black pepper

Boil the potatoes in lightly salted water until just done. Drain and leave until cool enough to handle.

Heat the oven to 200°C/gas mark 6. Heat the oil or fat to a depth of about 3mm in a large shallow roasting tin. Add enough potatoes to half cover the base. Bash the potatoes with a potato masher, just enough to break them. Turn in the hot oil, then sprinkle with fennel seed, salt and pepper.

Repeat with the rest of the potatoes in a second tin. Roast the potatoes for about 1 hour, until crusty and golden. Turn them occasionally, and rotate the trays, if you have to place one on a lower rack. putting the bottom to the top and so on. After about 40 minutes, if the potatoes are looking done, reduce the heat, or if they are looking pale, turn it up. Serve piled in a warm bowl with some flat-leaf parsley tucked in.

Tomatoes

Imagine life without tomatoes. No pizza, no ketchup, no red pasta sauce. But tomatoes are a relatively new addition to our culinary repertoire, only being widely accepted into our diet by the mid-eighteenth century.

The number of varieties available has burgeoned in the last few years, with heritage tomatoes vying for shelf space with new cultivars. There are striped ones, yellow ones, tiny pear-shaped ones, purple ones and even a velvety peach-skinned variety.

Each tomato has a subtly different flavour, texture and acidity level. Slice several different kinds and arrange them on a plate to make a salad, to really enjoy the various shapes and sizes. While it's great to have a range, and I am all for biodiversity, you will notice that novelty colours don't necessarily mean better eating qualities.

For my money, it's hard to do better than the large craggy tomato known as *Coeur de Boeuf* (Ox Heart) in France. It may be streaked with green at the stalk end (looks are not its strong point) but slice in and you'll find it is red all the way through – none of the insipid pale inside of second-rate tomatoes – with a complex structure of twisting ribs and channels. The flavour, naturally, is exceptional.

Ways with tomato

Skinning tomatoes

Peel tomatoes by dropping them into a bowl of boiling water, count to ten, then scoop them out with a slotted spoon. Rinse in cold water, then carefully pull the skin off. If the tomatoes are not very ripe, then they may need a few more seconds in the boiling water (just drop them back in the bowl) but don't leave them in until the skin splits and peels back. This is a sign that the flesh underneath is cooking, and it is a peeled tomato you are after, not a cooked, waterlogged one.

Storing tomatoes

In general, tomatoes should be kept out of the fridge, in a bowl on the kitchen table perhaps, where you can keep an eye on the colour as is deepens to perfect ripeness. Even those disappointing, hard, orange-red tomatoes can be coaxed to scarlet, and palatable ripeness, that way.

The only time I might consider keeping tomatoes in the fridge is if they are so ripe they are burstingly soft, on the point of going off. Then their best destination is a soup or sauce, and I'll put them in the vegetable drawer until I have a moment to make one – usually just by sweating a chopped onion (plus a finely chopped carrot and celery stick if I'm feeling fancy) in olive oil, adding the tomatoes and seasoning, including a little chilli, and cooking slowly to a pulpy mass. It can then be puréed with a hand blender and sieved, and thinned to a soup or sauce consistency with stock. The purée freezes well.

Tomato Salad

The best autumn tomato salad is made with just salt, olive oil and bread. Roughly chop the tomatoes (peel them first for a more elegant version), removing that hard white cone at the stalk end. Scoop into a bowl and sprinkle with sea salt flakes and a glug of good olive oil. Leave for 10 minutes or so, until the juices have run. Cut a thick slice of bread (I prefer white for this, ideally sourdough), toasting it if you like. Pile the tomatoes and their olive-oily juices on to the bread. Eat the savoury, juice-soaked bread with your fingers or a knife and fork if you prefer. You can, of course, dress it up with fresh herbs (chervil is very good, if you can get it, but any of the so-called soft herbs – basil, tarragon, dill, parsley, chives, coriander – work). Perhaps not mint though as to me the texture is wrong.

Monsieur Rouvière's Tomato Salad

This is the salad made by my friend Anne's father. He uses the tomatoes and onions that he grows in his garden in Sète in the south of France. His tomatoes are, as you would expect, deep red and well-flavoured. The onions are pure white ones, which are crisp and sweet to eat.

Chop 3–4 tomatoes roughly. Add 1 small white onion, chopped into the same sized pieces. Pour over 2 tablespoons olive oil, and add salt, pepper and a tiny splash of white wine vinegar.

Tomato and Onion Seed Chutney

This gorgeous chutney recipe, sweet as ketchup, is a simplified version of one given to me by Tom Bradbury, chef at the Kingswood Restaurant in Cornwall. The onion seed gives it a gorgeously nubbly texture, and it's so good I could eat it straight out of the jar. Make it with green or red tomatoes, or a mixture. Add half a teaspoonful each of coriander seed and fennel seed with the tomatoes if you wish. It's gorgeous with sausages and with cheese.

Makes 1 x 500ml jar

140ml cider or white wine
  vinegar

140g caster sugar

2 shallots, diced

1 garlic clove, crushed

500g tomatoes, washed and
  chopped

3 tablespoons tomato purée

50g sultanas

1 teaspoon chopped thyme

2 teaspoon black onion seed

Salt and freshly ground
  black pepper

Put the vinegar, sugar, shallots, garlic, 1 teaspoon of salt and a good grinding of pepper in a large saucepan. Bring the mixture gently to the boil and cook until it becomes syrupy.

Add the chopped tomatoes, the tomato purée and sultanas, and reduce the heat to a gentle simmer.

Cook until thick, then stir in the thyme and onion seed. Bottle in sterilised jars (see page 100). I keep my chutney in the fridge, where it lasts a month or more.

Morning After Slow-cooked Tomatoes with Bacon and Sourdough Toast

Burnt toast is a well-known hangover cure: it's supposed to absorb any alcohol still sloshing around. I prefer my carbon in these sticky, blackened tomatoes that taste delectably caramelised.

Heat a little olive oil in a non-stick frying pan and arrange halved tomatoes (2 per person), skin side down in it. Cook over a medium-low heat for about 10 minutes. Sprinkle with salt and turn over. Cook for another 30 minutes or so, until the juices have evaporated and the cut side of the tomatoes is dark and sticky. Eat the tomatoes piled on chunky toast, sourdough ideally, with bacon.

Semi-dried Tomatoes

Those leathery sun-dried tomatoes with their dusty caramel flavour have always left me cold: these are quite different. I first ate tomatoes like this, wrinkled and squishy, in the Victoria Market in Melbourne, when a stallholder passed one to me as I walked by. It was good salesmanship: that mouthful stopped me in my tracks. Intense, sweet and melting, it was the essence of tomato.

It is a good way to preserve a bumper crop of tomatoes, as semi-dried, they will keep for a few days in the fridge or for months in the freezer. Here's how I make them.

Semi-dried tomatoes are great in salads, mixed through a tumble of puy lentils and rocket, in tarts and gratins, in stews and sauces or in the canapé recipe on page 215.

Small, ripe tomatoes (up to 5cm across)

Preheat the oven to 140°C/gas mark 1.

Cut the tomatoes in half through their equator. Lay them cut side up on a baking tray and cook for 2–3 hours. Remove the tray from the oven when they look just a little wrinkled around the edges; they will shrink as they cool.

Tip

Use as they are or pack in jars, top up with olive oil and poke in a few sprigs of rosemary or thyme. Provided they are completely covered in oil, the tomatoes should last a couple of weeks stored in the fridge.

Squash

There are, as you may know, two kinds of squash: winter and summer. There are delicate-skinned, juicy summer ones we have rejoiced in (see page 136). Now it is the turn of winter squash. Rotund and fecund with tough skins and mature seeds, they are symbolic of autumn gluts.

Choosing…
- Check carefully and reject any with soft spots or broken skin before parting with any cash.
- Rough patches or spots of uneven colour generally indicate where the squash was resting on the ground, and are nothing to worry about.

- A pumpkin that seems light for its size will have a large cavity, making it good for carving, but don't expect great flavour from the flesh. It'll be perfect for the pumpkin cake recipe, though.
- Shiny skin may indicate an underripe squash or one that has been waxed, so pick a matt one.

... and using squash
- Don't automatically **peel** a squash. The skin may be edible once cooked, or at least easier to remove. If it must be stripped, then a sharp vegetable peeler is the most efficient tool for all but the toughest skin.
- Try to use it **all at once**, or keep leftovers wrapped and in the fridge ready to use the following day. Once cut, winter squash don't keep well.
- To **roast** squash, cut it into wedges and turn in oil, then arrange on a baking sheet skin side down for maximum browning. Roast at 200°C/gas mark 6 for 20–30 minutes until soft through.
- For a **purée**, peel, then steam the squash until soft or boil it in the minimum of water. Mash and drain in a sieve for 5 minutes or so before mixing with butter, salt and lots of pepper.
- To **pan-fry**, slice thinly and cook over a high heat in a mixture of oil and butter until touched with brown.
- **Flavours** that squash loves: nutmeg, sage, thyme, black pepper, ginger and chilli.

The Squash Squadron

HOKKAIDO SQUASH – distinctive squat cylindrical shape like a tin of furniture polish with a deep orange skin.
Good to eat? Yellow-orange flesh with a strong scent and flavour of cucumber.
How to use: Crunchy carrot-like texture means it can be eaten raw, sliced in salads. Or slice it thinly and pan-fry. Roasts to a pleasantly starchy, mild sweet potato flavour.

MUSQUE DE PROVENCE – large and deep ridged, but with a thin skin, which comes in a number of colours from orange through pale green to dark green.
Good to eat? Mild and sweet, very juicy. A little fibrous.
How to use: Can be eaten raw, thinly sliced, or pan-fried. Surprisingly for such a juicy squash, it roasts well too, turning starchy.

CROWN PRINCE – a beautiful pale blue-green colour, with a squat, heavily ridged shape.
Good to eat? Dense and starchy, almost potato-like with no fibres. Lovely sweet-chestnut flavour.
How to use: Roast in olive oil with herbs and garlic, or purée in soups.

ACORN – pointy-shaped squash that comes in lots of colours, with pale flesh.
Good to eat? Pleasant nutty flavour, a little mealy but still a bit juicy.
How to use: A well-balanced squash that is good in almost any squash dish.

BLUE BALLET – the same beautiful colour as Crown Prince, but with a bulbous onion shape.
Good to eat? Very starchy, but less sweet or distinctive tasting than Crown Prince.
How to use: roast in a mix with other squash, or as potato substitute. Makes a good soup.

KABUCHI – a flat onion-shaped squash, dark green with subtle pale stripes.
Good to eat? Dryish flesh with a mild aromatic flavour.
How to use: Roast with crushed cumin seeds or purée in soups.

BUTTERNUT – immediately recognisable by its palest tan skin and elongated shape.
Good to eat? Ultra-sweet, like a sweet potato, a little fibrous, juicy. Probably the finest flavour of all.
How to use: Good for any purpose, but be wary of that sweetness, which may need tempering with salt, lime juice or chilli.

HARLEQUIN – pointed like an acorn squash, but with a tender, striped skin.
Good to eat? A high water content and a mild flavour.
How to use: Better sliced and sautéd than roasted, which makes it mushy, much like a courgette.

TURK'S TURBAN – distinctive looking with its striped topknot, it has incredibly hard skin, making it difficult to cut.
Good to eat? Starchy with a mild flavour.
How to use: Make the most of the beautiful shape by hollowing it out to use as a tureen for soup, although you will need a strong arm to do that. Or cut into chunks and use in the risotto.

MUNCHKIN – tiny, squat little pumpkin with a fairly soft skin.
Good to eat? Nothing to write home about, but pleasant enough.
How to use: the size and shape are the thing, so not one for a purée. Cut into wedges and roast, or scoop out the seeds and bake whole with a pat of butter in the cavity. Pretty as tea light holders too.

Roast Winter Squash, Red Peppers, Red Onions and Sausages

My friend Caroline Gilmartin gave me this recipe for a gorgeous savoury mêlée of sausages and vegetables. The sticky, savoury juices at the bottom of the pan are particularly good, so scrape the dish well as you serve up. Serve with mashed potatoes or just good bread.

Serves 4

8 large, best-quality sausages

2 red peppers, deseeded and cut into chunks

2 medium red onions, peeled and quartered

1kg winter squash such as butternut, deseeded and cut into wedges about 2.5cm thick

Leaves from 3 rosemary sprigs

Olive oil

Salt

Preheat the oven to 200°C/gas mark 6.

Put the sausages, peppers, red onions and squash in a large roasting tin.

Scatter over the rosemary, along with a fat pinch of salt. Drizzle with 2–3 tablespoons olive oil and turn the sausages and vegetables in it until well coated.

Roast for about 40 minutes until the sausages are cooked through and the vegetables are tender and browned.

Pumpkin Soup

Pumpkins and squash make beautifully creamy, light-textured soup. Tart it up for a party with sage leaves, fried in hot oil until they turn a deep, bright green edged with brown. Drain them on kitchen paper (they'll crisp up) and scatter over the soup.

I'm assuming that you are going to use your pumpkin either to make a lantern for Halloween or as a tureen for soup but if that is not your plan, you could get away with a smaller pumpkin, or a slice out of a huge one, by cutting it into chunks and peeling away the skin with a vegetable peeler.

Serves 6 (makes about 1.8 litres)

1 football-sized pumpkin (around 3kg, giving about 1kg flesh)

50g butter

1 large onion, sliced

2 celery sticks, sliced

1 red chilli, chopped (see tip)

1 garlic clove, chopped

1 litre chicken or vegetable stock

200g smoked brie, roughly chopped (remove the rind first)

Salt and freshly ground black pepper

Cut a lid from the top of the pumpkin. Pull out the seeds (keep them for roasting), then with a sturdy metal spoon or ice-cream scoop, scrape out the flesh from the inside, until you are left with a thin shell.

Melt the butter in a large pan and add the onion, celery and chilli. Cook gently for 10 minutes or so until soft and melting.

Add the garlic and cook for a further minute, then stir in the pumpkin flesh. Cover and cook for 10 minutes, then remove the lid and simmer until all the liquid has cooked away, leaving the vegetables sizzling in the butter.

Pour in the stock and liquidise in a blender or food-processor. Add enough water to make a pouring cream consistency, and bring to simmering point.

Taste and season with salt and pepper. Pour into the pumpkin shell and serve, adding a few cubes of smoked brie to each serving.

Tip

Chilli heat varies enormously, so much so that even two from the same plant can range from mild to mouth-searingly powerful. Nibble a scrap before adding it all to the pan, and use more or less accordingly.

Pumpkin Cake with Pomegranate

My Boston-based sister-in-law introduced me to pumpkin cake, a moist, mildly spiced delight in the tradition of carrot cake. It is well-behaved too, baking happily in a round tin, a loaf tin or as a tray bake (great for bonfire parties). The icing is optional, but the juicy, sherbet tang of pomegranate seeds is a great foil for the rich creaminess.

To make an easy almost-store cupboard cake, use a tin of pumpkin purée instead of the cooked fresh pumpkin.

675g wedge of pumpkin or pumpkin flesh

120g butter

225g caster sugar

2 eggs, lightly beaten

1 teaspoon vanilla essence

2 teaspoons mixed spice

225g self-raising flour

Cream cheese icing (see below)

Seeds from 1 pomegranate

Preheat the oven to 180°C/gas mark 4.

Grease and line a 20cm round cake tin or a 22cm square traybake tin or a 500g loaf tin.

Chop the pumpkin flesh and put it in a pan with half a cupful of water. Bring to the boil, cover tightly, and cook gently for 10–15 minutes until the pumpkin is very soft. Stir often and check that it is not sticking, adding a tiny bit more water if necessary.

Take off the lid and mash the pumpkin to a purée. Stir it over a medium heat until any extra liquid has evaporated. Tip the purée into a sieve suspended over a bowl and leave to cool.

Cream the butter and caster sugar together until light and fluffy. Whisk in the eggs a little at a time, followed by the vanilla and spice.

Weigh out 225g of the pumpkin purée and stir it into the creamed mixture. (The remaining purée can be used in soups or heated with butter and eaten with sausages.) Fold in the flour.

Scrape the mixture into the greased, lined tin and bake for 45 minutes for a round tin or traybake, 1 hour and 10 minutes for a loaf cake. Check that the cake is done by pushing a skewer into the middle. It should come out clean.

Cool for 10 minutes in the tin, then turn out to finish cooling on a rack. Ice the cake with Cream Cheese Icing (see below), and sprinkle with pomegranate seeds.

Cream Cheese Icing

100g cream cheese

50g butter

250g icing sugar

1 teaspoon vanilla essence

1 teaspoon grated orange zest and 1 tablespoon juice

Beat the cream cheese with the butter until smooth. Whisk in the sugar, vanilla essence and the grated orange zest and juice. If the mixture is very soft, chill it in the fridge until firm enough to spread.

Pears, Plums and Greengages

Keats was bang on when he called autumn the 'season of mists and mellow fruitfulness'. If there is ever a glut, it is now. Friends and neighbours with trees bring round plums, apples and pears, so my biggest bowls are filled with fruit. Then it is a race to use them all before they start to go brown and are wasted.

We have cakes and tarts and salads, and then rules about sweet and savoury start to be broken as fruit sneaks into main courses. I add plums to the roasting tin when cooking pork belly, where they collapse to a tangy sauce, and apples to the celeriac and walnut salad on page 188.

Most of all, though, I eat autumn fruit with cheese. There is something about the sweetness of a Conference with salty, bitter blue cheese, or a smooth Comice pear with salty, grainy Parmesan, or a honey-sweet greengage with a creamy white cheese and more honey. Blissfully easy, and fantastically good.

Pear and Rocket Salad with Blue Cheese

Pear and blue cheese is a fine combination, the sweetness of the fruit mellowing the salty, bitter cheese. Eat this salad as a first course or instead of a cheese course at the end of a meal.

Serves 2–3

1 ripe pear (Conference, Williams or Concorde)

Handful of rocket leaves

2 tablespoons olive oil

1 teaspoon sherry vinegar

30g or so blue cheese, something mild and creamy (I like Blacksticks Blue)

Salt and freshly ground black pepper

Slice the pear across into thin rounds. No need, for once, to remove the rasping skin or the barely there core.

Toss with the rocket leaves in a bowl. Beat together the olive oil, vinegar and a pinch of salt and grinding of pepper, and toss together with the rocket leaves and pear.

Use a potato peeler to shave in scraps of blue cheese. Serve straight away.

Greengages with Fresh Cheese and Honey

Although I use greengages, this combination is delicious with any soft-textured fruit from the *Prunus* family – peaches and apricots, in particular, but ordinary plums are good too, as are non-plum figs and pears. The choice of cheese is harder – a young Pecorino is good, but so is a very fresh young goats' cheese or a simple curd cheese. As for the honey, that ridiculously overpriced jar I bought on holiday suddenly seems worth every penny, once trickled fragrantly over the top.

Serves 4–6

500g ripe greengages

150g or so fresh cheese

runny flower honey

Halve the fruit and remove the stones. Slice the cheese, or break it up as best you can if it is very soft. Scatter the fruit over and around, then trickle over the honey

Ginger Poached Pears

Pears infused with both fresh and preserved ginger, and trickled with chocolate are sublime and this is a wonderful way of using up a glut. They can be made up to a week ahead and kept covered, in their syrup, in the fridge, or frozen.

Serves 6

1 x 240g jar stem ginger

6 small, firm pears, peeled

1 tablespoon (firmly packed) finely grated fresh ginger

Squeeze of lemon juice and a wisp of lemon zest

TO SERVE

100g dark chocolate, melted

whipped cream or ice cream

Thinly slice the balls of stem ginger. Put them in a smallish pan with the pears, the syrup from the jar, 300ml water, the grated ginger, lemon juice and the zest.

Bring to simmering point and poach very gently for about 1 hour, turning the fruit occasionally.

When the fruit is very tender (the exact timing will vary), turn off the heat and leave the pears to cool in the syrup.

Serve the pears with a trickle of melted chocolate, a little of the syrup and lightly whipped cream or ice cream.

A Proper Plum Tart

A proper tart, like something out of a French pâtisserie window, finishes a meal with a flourish and is satisfyingly straightforward to make. Pastry is key to a good tart, but the crumbly, flaky pastry, made with lard or white fat and so good in pies, is not right here. A crisp, biscuity texture and buttery flavour are best, so choose a rich, sweet pastry recipe made with butter and egg yolk. If it has to be ready-made, select an all-butter version and roll it out on icing sugar instead of flour.

Serves 8–10

Rich, sweet shortcrust pastry
    (see opposite)

FOR THE FILLING

100g ground almonds (grind
    whole blanched almonds
    in a food-processor for
    the best flavour)

100g butter at room
    temperature (unsalted is
    best, but salted is fine)

85g caster sugar

1 large egg

1 tablespoon plain flour

1 tablespoon kirsch (see
    page 90, or brandy, almond
    liqueur or orange juice)

700g plums, halved and
    stoned

4 tablespoons apricot or
    plum jam

Squeeze of lemon juice

Unless you are using ready-made, first make your pastry. Use it to line a 25cm loose-based tart tin and place in the fridge to chill.

Preheat the oven to 200°C/gas mark 6, placing a large baking sheet on the middle shelf to heat up.

Beat together the almonds, butter and sugar. Mix in the egg, flour and kirsch. Spread the mixture over the base of the pastry tart case. Top the almond cream with the halved plums (cut side down).

Put the tart in the oven on the hot baking sheet and bake for 12–15 minutes, until the pastry is beginning to brown, then lower the temperature to 170°C/gas mark 3 and cook for a further 40 minutes to 1 hour, until the filling is set and lightly browned.

Check the tart after 30 minutes, and cover the edges of the pastry if they are getting too brown. The best way to do this is to take a sheet of greaseproof paper or foil. Cut a circle out of the middle about 20cm across. Lay the frame you've made over the tart, so that the pastry is covered but the filling is visible.

If your plums were very ripe and juicy, they may release so much liquid that the tart seems soggy. In that case, continue to bake it until it is dry and set, up to a further 30 minutes or so. As long as you have covered the edges it will come to no harm.

Remove from the oven and leave the tart to cool in the tin.

Meanwhile, put the jam in a small pan with a squeeze of lemon juice. Heat gently until runny, then sieve out the lumps before brushing the glaze liberally over the cooled tart.

Sweet Shortcrust Pastry

**Makes enough to line
a 25cm tart tin**

125g unsalted butter
225g plain flour mixed with
  a pinch of salt
1 small egg, beaten
75g caster sugar
1 teaspoon vanilla extract

Rub the butter into the flour and salt (or you can do this in a food-processor). Add the egg, sugar and vanilla extract to the bowl. Combine to form a dough.

Turn out of the bowl, pat into a round, cover with clingfilm and refrigerate for at least an hour before rolling out to line a loose-based tart tin. Chill again, covered with clingfilm, for a further hour before baking.

Pastry tips

Rolling out pastry

Always roll forward, never at an angle. Turn the pastry rather than the pin, using a flexible bladed metal palette knife to loosen the pastry if it sticks to the work surface.

Pastry needs to be rolled to an even thickness to cook evenly

If you aren't practised in this, buy narrow strips of wood (each around 5cm wide) one 0.5cm thick, another 0.25cm each, cut into 2 × 30cm lengths (a builders' merchant or DIY shop should oblige). Place one under each end of the rolling pin as you roll, making it impossible to roll thinner that the wooden strips. This sounds a faff, but I promise it's worth it – it makes rolling accurately so much easier and faster.

If the pastry is very sticky

Roll it between two sheets of clingfilm. Peel off the top layer, and invert the pastry into the tart tin. Ease the pastry into place, and then peel off the second sheet of clingfilm.

When lining a tart tin

Try not to stretch the pastry to make it fit as it tends to shrink back to its original size when baked.

To bake blind

Preheat the oven to 200°C/gas mark 6. Prick the base of the pastry-lined tart tin all over with a fork and line with baking parchment or foil. Weigh it down with beans, coins (I keep a jar of old foreign coins for the purpose) or ceramic baking beans, which conduct the heat better than ordinary beans. Push them in to the edges as far as possible. Bake for 10 minutes, then lift out the foil or paper with the beans or coins, and bake for a further 10 minutes of so until the pastry is dry and lightly coloured.

My Cheatin' Tart

Really this 'tart' is no more than apples-on-toast, baked in the oven. They become unbelievably good, with a crisp buttery base, soft sweet apples and caramelised topping. Put them together in less than a minute and bake them while you eat the main course.

Per person

1 thick slice of good white bread

Butter

1–2 tablespoons demerara sugar

1 tablespoon ground almonds

A few thin slices of apple

Preheat the oven to 180°C/gas mark 4.

Butter the bread generously on both sides. Lay the slices on a baking tray and sprinkle with half the sugar. Press the apple slices on top, fanning them out. Sprinkle with the ground almonds and the rest of the sugar. Dot with a little more butter.

Bake for 30 minutes until golden and bubbling. Allow to cool for 5 minutes (or you'll burn your mouth) before serving with cream or custard (see opposite).

Peach Leaf or Vanilla Custard

A proper egg-based custard is a thing of joy. Vanilla is the classic flavouring, but instead when I can get hold of peach leaves from a friend's tree I infuse the hot milk with them for 20 minutes, then strain it before adding the egg yolk. It gives the sauce a delicate almond flavour, which goes particularly well with the apple tarts. A spoonful of amaretto-type liqueur stirred in at the end works well if you cannot source peach leaves.

Serves 4–6

300ml milk

1 vanilla pod, split
   lengthways

1 egg yolk

1 teaspoon sugar

Heat the milk to just below boiling point. Scrape some of the seeds out of the vanilla pod and add them to the milk, along with the pod. Leave to infuse for 20 minutes, then remove the pod (rinse it briefly and leave it to dry, then store it in your sugar jar to flavour the sugar).

Whisk the egg yolk into the warm milk with the sugar, then cook over a very low heat, stirring all the time, until the mixture thickens noticeably (which it does when it reaches about 78°C, should you have a sugar thermometer). The change is quite marked, and fast, a matter of seconds as the mixture becomes thin cream rather than simple milk-with-a-bit-of-egg-yolk texture. Don't let it boil or the mixture will scramble, but a few cooked strands are an indication you are getting close to the right temperature, as the vestiges of egg white still attached to the yolk coagulate at a lower temperature than the egg yolk.

An Autumn Mezze

The early autumn glut of aubergines, peppers and tomatoes is the moment to pull together a Turkish-inspired mezze. The snacking, sharing style is good for lunch, and even better in the evening. You can make it all ahead for an after-theatre or after-pub supper, but do take everything out of the fridge before you go out. The dishes should be at a mellow room temperature, not teeth-chillingly cold. Serve with warm flat breads or pitta bread, and bowls of olive oil for dipping.

Other things to add to a mezze:

- A bowl of sparklingly fresh, carefully washed vegetables: radishes, peppers, gem lettuces, tomatoes, spring onions.

- Hot pitta or flat bread.

- Feta cheese or Turkish *peynir* (another sheep's milk cheese), sliced, and sprinkled with grated lemon zest and olive oil.

- **Plum and tomato salad** – not especially Middle Eastern, but good with the other dishes nonetheless. Slice tomatoes and stoned plums and arrange them on a plate together. Sprinkle with a little salt, sherry vinegar and olive oil and top with a few basil leaves.

Cucumber with Goats' Yogurt and Mint

A cooling salad, similar to Greek *tsatziki* or Turkish *cacik*. Some people grate the cucumber, but chopping it doesn't take long and makes for a much better texture. Goats' yogurt has a delicious mild goats' cheese flavour, but you could use ordinary Greek yogurt instead.

Serves 4 as part of a mezze

1 large cucumber

200ml goats' yogurt

1 tiny garlic clove, crushed (optional)

6 mint sprigs, leaves only, chopped

Salt and freshly ground black pepper

Peel the cucumber and cut it in half lengthways. Scoop out the seeds with a teaspoon. (I eat them as a cook's perk, but you could juice them or purée them into a gazpacho.) Cut the cucumber into pea-sized cubes.

Put the cucumber in a colander and sprinkle with ½ teaspoon salt. Leave to drain for about 30 minutes.

Rinse the cucumber and dry it in a tea towel. Mix with the yogurt and garlic (if you are using it). Season with pepper.

Just before serving, chop the mint and mix it in. Serve in a small bowl.

Aubergine Salad, Turkish style

This salad of chopped aubergine is inspired by a Turkish dish called *Patlican salatasi* (aubergine purée). Grilling the aubergine in a naked flame until charred gives this dip its delicious flavour, but if you don't have gas you could roast the aubergine under a grill instead. In that case, it won't taste so smoky, so add a pinch of smoked paprika (available from delis and larger supermarkets) to make up.

Serves 4 as part of a mezze

2 small aubergines

2 tablespoons oil

Juice of ½ a lemon

1 tiny garlic clove

3 tablespoons plain yogurt (optional)

Salt

Spear one of the aubergines with a long-handled fork and hold it in a gas flame, turning occasionally, until completely blackened. You can leave it lying on the flame for a few seconds if necessary, but keep a close eye on it. Repeat with the other aubergine. Leave them to cool.

Pull off as much of the blackened skin as you can, then rinse briefly under a tap to remove the rest. Chop the flesh, sprinkle with a pinch of salt and leave in a colander to drain for a few minutes.

Mix the aubergine with the lemon juice, oil and garlic. Add the yogurt if you like, which will make the dish creamy and milder, useful if the aubergine has a strong flavour. Pile into a small bowl and serve with pitta bread.

Borek Filled with Spinach, Raisins and Pine Nuts

Spinach is usually paired with feta in these triangular pastries, but to boost the flavour, I've stolen from the classic Moorish trio of spinach, raisins and pine nuts – a divine combination that has influenced the cuisine of Sicily and the Catalan region of Spain. Any leftover are great for lunchboxes.

Makes 12

FOR THE FILLING

2 tablespoons olive oil

400g spinach, washed

1 red onion, finely sliced

1 teaspoon ground cinnamon

4 tablespoons raisins

1 tablespoon pine nuts, toasted

Salt and freshly ground black pepper

FOR THE BOREK

1 x 270g pack filo pastry

4 tablespoons walnut oil or melted butter

2 tablespoons poppy seeds

Preheat the oven to 220°C/gas mark 7 and lightly grease a baking tray.

First make the filling. Heat 1 tablespoon of the oil in a large pan and add the spinach. Cover and cook, stirring occasionally, until the spinach has wilted.

Drain in a sieve then tip the spinach into the centre of a clean tea towel and squeeze it dry, twisting the towel until you have a tennis ball of compacted leaves. Chop the spinach.

Heat the second tablespoon of oil in a small pan and add the onion. Cook until softened.

Stir in the cinnamon, cook for a few seconds, then leave to cool before mixing with the spinach, raisins and pine nuts. Taste and adjust the seasoning.

Unroll the filo pastry and cut the stack of sheets in half lengthways, so that each stack measures about 22 × 11cm. Cover the pile with a sheet of clingfilm to stop it drying out.

Lay one piece of filo lengthways on the work surface and brush it with walnut oil or melted butter. Lay another piece on top.

Put a heaped tablespoon of the spinach mixture near the left end of the pastry strip. Fold the pastry diagonally over the filling, by bringing the bottom left-hand corner up to the top to create a filled triangle. Keep folding the pastry over and over, enclosing the filling in a samosa-like parcel.

Lay the wrapped borek on the baking tray, bending in the ends to form a crescent shape if you like. Brush with more oil or butter and sprinkle with poppy seeds. Repeat with the rest of the pastry and filling.

Bake for 7–10 minutes until brown and crisp. Cool on a rack. Serve warm or at room temperature.

Peppers with Turkish Tarator

Food nomenclature can get very confusing. What the British call chicory, in France is endive, and vice versa. The Americans talk about corn, which is what the Brits think of as sweetcorn, and what they call corn, the Yanks call wheat. Lolly in Australia, meanwhile, is any kind of sweetie or candy, while to me, British to the core, a lolly is something on a stick.

But I digress. *Tarator* is what we have here. In the Balkans that would mean a chilled cucumber soup, and in many Middle Eastern countries *tarator* is a sesame sauce or dip. But this is a Turkish-style mezze, and this is what (I hope) a Turk would recognise as *tarator*, that's to say a nubbly, savoury sauce made with walnuts and bread.

Usually served with fish (try it with red mullet) it's excellent with grilled peppers too. To eat this as a starter, gently mix the pepper strips with a handful of wild rocket and top each helping with a little *tarator*.

Serves 4 as a starter or part of a mezze

4 peppers (red, yellow and orange)

6 tablespoons olive oil

50g white or brown bread (remove the crusts before weighing)

1 garlic clove, roughly chopped

50g shelled walnuts

1 teaspoon red or white wine vinegar

Coriander leaves

Salt and freshly ground black pepper

Cut the peppers in half and pull out the seeds, membranes and stalk. Press down flat, then grill, skin side up, until blistered and patched with black.

Put them in a bowl and cover with a plate. Leave to cool, then strip off all the skin.

Cut the flesh into strips. Toss with 2 tablespoons olive oil and leave to one side.

Tear the bread into chunks and put in a food-processor with the garlic. Whizz to crumbs, then add the walnuts and process again until the walnuts are ground. Add the rest of the olive oil, and process again.

With the motor running, pour in 4 tablespoons of water and the vinegar. Add a little more water if necessary to make a soft spooning consistency. Taste and season with salt and pepper.

Arrange the peppers on a plate. Dollop on some of the *tarator* and scatter with coriander leaves. Serve the rest of the *tarator* in a separate bowl.

Parsley and Bulgur Wheat Salad

Outside the Middle East, bulgur wheat salads called tabouleh are often a buff-coloured mounds flecked with herbs. I prefer the reverse, as they are made in Arabia, a salad of herbs speckled with grains of wheat. Lemon sour balancing the ferric kick of the parsley, it is uniquely refreshing. Make it half a day ahead if it suits you, and store it in the fridge. The bulgur will absorb more of the flavours.

Serves 4 as part of a mezze

1 tablespoon bulgur wheat

2 large bunches (around 150g) flat-leaf parsley

1 small bunch (around 20g) fresh mint

3 tomatoes, deseeded and chopped into pea-size pieces

3 spring onions, finely chopped

2 tablespoons lemon juice

4 tablespoons olive oil

Ground cinnamon

Salt and freshly ground black pepper

Rinse the bulgur wheat very well, drain and set to one side to soak up the remaining moisture.

Wash the herbs and chop them, removing the tough stalks (save the parsley stalks for stock, in the freezer if necessary). Don't chop too finely – the pieces should be no smaller than a grain of rice and some will be pea-size.

Mix the herbs, tomatoes, spring onions, bulgur wheat, lemon juice and olive oil. Season with salt, pepper and a pinch of ground cinnamon.

Other grains and starches that work in salads

I can't get excited about cold rice, but all these are much more interesting:

Couscous

Not a grain at all but tiny beads of pasta. The authentic way to cook them involves soaking and steaming, but for a salad just measure a cupful into a bowl and pour over an equal volume of boiling water or stock. Cover and leave to stand for 5 minutes, then fluff up with a fork.

Israeli Couscous or *Ptitim*

Great fat balls of pasta, a Brobdingnagian couscous, these give an interesting heft to salads. They need cooking for 10–12 minutes in stock or water before using. For a toasted flavour, fry them in a little olive oil first until golden brown.

Pearled Spelt

Spelt is an ancient form of wheat that some people find more digestible than modern varieties. Simmer it in stock for 30 minutes, until tender, then drain. It gives a nutty, chewy quality to salads, and is best with gutsy flavours such as olives, parsley and walnuts. Use *faro* (Italian pearled wheat) and pearled barley in the same way.

Quinoa

A South American seed, quinoa (pronounced *keen*-wah) is high in protein and gluten free, with a similar texture to couscous. Simmer it in boiling water for 10 minutes, until you can just see a tiny sprout lifting away from the seed. Use in the same way as couscous.

Late Autumn

After the harvest the riot of produce settles down to a simpler repertoire. Where I live the first hard frosts sweeten the parsnips and mellow the kale, and those doll's house cabbages – Brussels sprouts – are tight-budded on the stem. And proper, homegrown onions are at their finest: firm-fleshed and fresh tasting.

Best of all is the game. Eating wild meat, even if it has been initially reared in captivity such as pheasant, is amongst the most guilt-free of meats and would have been familiar to our ancestors. Not that early man would have had our battery of spices and alcohol to mellow the powerful flavours of untamed animals.

I still want salads, but they must be crisp cold-weather ingredients that have the resilience to cope with frosts and chill, unlike the fragile salads of summer. Squeaky, satiny chicory, jewel-bright pomegranate seeds and crunchy slices of Jerusalem artichoke all fit the bill. I'll sneak in some fresh herbs too, cosseted in a warm corner of the garden or else imported, and very glad of them I am too.

As for puddings, there is time for hot cooked tarts and pies with the later apples and the quinces, and ice creams are surprisingly good now too, made in autumnal flavours such as hazelnut.

Comfort Soups

Soup is the one food group (I use the term loosely) that I could live on indefinitely. Warming, hydrating and so simple to eat, babying the eater with soft textures. And who doesn't find it soothing to eat from a single bowl with a spoon?

I've lost count of the virtues of soup. A bit of texture, bits and bobs floating temptingly in broth or chunks of vegetable in a creamy purée, turns them into a proper meal. They are thrifty and little trouble to make, and most reheat well, so there is no problem using the leftovers. Most soups are vegetable-rich, and so eating plenty should help stave off colds and bugs too.

The simplest soup starts with just a leek, fried in butter. Add a chopped potato, seasoning and cover with water and simmer until the potato is soft. Thin with a little milk, until the texture is right for you, purée it if you like, and eat from a deep bowl.

This formula is a great place to start if you want to make a quick soup from your veg box vegetables or what you have in the fridge. Just add them along with the potato, adjusting the quantity of leek and spud according to the starchiness of what you are bringing to the pot.

Here are some other ideas, all infinitely adaptable.

Root and Ginger Soup

Too often the swede or turnip is watery and acrid. In fact, it makes a good side vegetable, boiled until tender but not collapsing, and well buttered. Don't steam it, as the insistent earthy, resinous quality of the raw vegetable needs the dilution of a pan of boiling water. Best of all, make this soup. The spicy ginger turns swede into a warm, fragrant pleasure, not sexy, perhaps, but very comforting.

Serves 4

2 tablespoons olive oil

1 onion, chopped

1 swede, the size of a large grapefruit

2 medium potatoes, diced

1.2 litres good chicken stock

1–2 tablespoons grated fresh ginger

Salt

Heat the oil in a large pan and add the onion. While it cooks slowly, prepare the other vegetables. Peel the swede (a potato peeler is the best tool for the job) and cut it into dice. Dice the potato too, although no need to peel it unless it has a particularly tough or rough skin.

When the onion is soft and translucent (this will take 10 minutes) add the swede and potato. Stir well and cook for another couple of minutes.

Stir in the stock and a good pinch of salt. Add the ginger a little at a time, tasting the stock until it has a gentle gingery kick.

Simmer until the vegetables are soft, adding a bit more water if necessary.

With a hand blender, purée the soup briefly, just enough to thicken the liquid but leaving some chunks. (Or purée the lot if you prefer a smooth soup.) Taste to check the seasoning and serve.

Beef Cheek, Barley and Tomato Soup

A hefty main course soup for a cold day, that's wonderful eaten with bread and cheese. When browning the meat, don't be tempted to crowd it into the pan to do it all at once. The meat will steam, turning a greyish beige, rather than caramelising to a delicious savouriness.

Serves 4

2 tablespoons olive oil

500g beef cheek or shin, cut into 2cm chunks

1 large onion, chopped

2 cloves garlic, crushed

75g pearled barley or spelt

a bay leaf

2 x 400g tins of tomatoes

300ml red wine

1 litre beef stock or water

salt and freshly ground black pepper

Heat 1 tablespoon of olive oil in a large pan. Add a few cubes of beef, so that they are well spaced over the base of the pan. (If they are too close, they won't brown.) Cook, turning occasionally, until well browned, to a deep mahogany, on at least 3 sides. Scoop out and repeat with the rest of the meat, adding more oil if necessary.

Return all the meat to the pan. Add the onion and cook for ten minutes, until soft. Add the garlic and cook for another minute.

Stir in the wine and let it bubble up, then add the barley or spelt, bay leaf, tomatoes, stock or water, salt and pepper. Simmer very gently for 1½ to 2 hours, until the meat is very tender and the tomatoes have collapsed. Taste and check the seasoning, and serve in deep bowls.

Hot and Sour Noodle Soup

A great soup to lift the spirits. The chilli gives an endorphin rush, the lime juice clears the sinuses and the ginger wards off colds. Add extra chilli if you are a hot-food addict. Some protein, here chicken or prawns, gives the dish main course status, but on a cold night I'd be just as happy to eat it without either.

Serves 4, or 2 as a main course

700ml chicken or prawn stock

Thumb-size piece fresh ginger, grated

1–2 red chillies, finely sliced

3 tablespoons lime juice

2 tablespoons fish sauce (*nam pla* or *nuoc nam*)

200g large raw prawns, or some slivers of raw chicken (optional)

60g fine rice noodles, cooked and rinsed in cold water

Small bunch of fresh coriander

Heat the stock in a pan with the ginger and a few slices of chilli, simmering very gently for 5–10 minutes. Strain into a clean pan and stir in the lime juice and fish sauce. Add the prawns or chicken to the stock now and cook for about 3 minutes, until cooked through. Stir in the noodles and divide between four bowls. Top with coriander leaves and the rest of the chilli.

Prawn stock

If you are buying whole prawns, use the heads and shells to make an intensely flavoured stock. Chop 1 onion, 1 celery stick, some parsley stalks (I save them in a bag in the freezer for stock, along with Florence fennel trimmings). Put them in a pan with a little oil and cook until soft. Add a bay leaf and the prawn heads, cover with water and simmer for 30 minutes. Strain and use immediately, or cool then freeze for up to a month.

Too much faff? Your stock will still be worth having if you just chuck the prawn heads in a pan with a pinch of crushed fennel seed, cover with water and simmer for 30 minutes.

Chicken and Coconut Soup with Basil and Chilli Oil

This soup is quite lovely, a soothing, pure white broth with tender chunks of poached chicken and soft basil leaves. I love it trickled with the flame-red chilli oil.

Serves 2–3 as a main course

4 tablespoons sunflower oil

½ teaspoon paprika

2 large mild red chillies, chopped

400ml coconut milk

600ml chicken stock

2 tablespoons grated fresh ginger

2 lemongrass stalks, tough outer leaves discarded, the rest chopped

2 chicken breasts, skinned and cut into large dice

250g egg noodles, cooked and rinsed in cold water

Leaves from a small bunch of fresh basil

Salt

Heat the oil in a small pan and add the paprika and chilli. Cook gently, stirring occasionally, for 5 minutes, until the chilli is soft. Rub through a sieve and keep the deep orange oil to one side.

Put the coconut milk, stock, ginger and lemongrass in a large pan and bring to simmering point. Allow to infuse for 10 minutes, then strain. Return to the rinsed-out pan, and add the chicken. Simmer very gently for 5 minutes or so, until the chicken is cooked through. Stir in the noodles and heat through, then add the basil. Taste and add salt if necessary, before serving trickled with the chilli oil.

Four cold-weather salads

- Peel and slice Jerusalem artichokes into coin-thick slices. Dress with olive oil and mix with thinly sliced shallots, shavings of Parmesan and parsley leaves. Season with salt, pepper and a squeeze of lemon juice.

- Mix slices of *mooli* or young turnips with segments of orange, pitted black olives and thin slices of red onion. Dress with orange juice and olive oil.

- Shave carrots into ribbons with a vegetable peeler and dress with lemon juice and walnut oil. Leave to macerate for a couple of hours, then add a few chopped walnuts and chopped parsley just before serving.

- Toss 50g pecan nuts in a hot frying pan with a teaspoonful of honey and a pinch of salt, until they caramelise. Make a dressing of 1 teaspoon honey, 2 teaspoons sherry vinegar and 4 tablespoons olive oil, salt and pepper. Toss together with the nuts, a handful of bitter winter leaves (frisée, say, or radicchio) and roasted chunks of parsnip.

Root Vegetables

Growing secretly beneath the ground, there is magic to root vegetables, amongst the sweetest of the true vegetables. One root vegetable even produces much of the world's sugar – the humble beet.

Roots store well, and while I like to buy mine with foliage on as proof of their freshness, it is best to cut these off straight away as the leaves sap away at the goodness in the root, so it eventually becomes soft. You can always use the leaves from beetroot as you would spinach. Soil, however, is another matter. A coating of soil on a vegetable might not be as appealing as those scrubbed vegetables in their plastic bags in the supermarket, but it protects the root from light and reduces moisture loss. Leave the vegetables in their muddy coats until you are ready to use them.

We tend to automatically reach for a saucepan or roasting tin for our root veg. Don't forget, though, that many of the vegetables we generally cook are good eaten raw as well, sweet, but crunchy, nutty and peppery too. The deep hue of beetroot, peeled and grated, makes a dramatic addition to a simple salad or side dish.

Jerusalem Artichoke Gratin

This artichoke take on potatoes *dauphinoise* is supremely delicious with roast beef or guinea fowl (see page 172). Rich, but worth it.

1kg Jerusalem artichokes, preferably the Fuseau variety

About 300ml whipping or double cream

Salt and freshly ground black pepper

Preheat the oven to 180°C/gas mark 4.

Peel and slice the artichokes as thick as a coin. (Wear gloves – the artichokes stain your hands an unappealing grey.) Arrange the slices in overlapping rows in a buttered ovenproof dish. Season well between each layer.

Pour over enough cream, not to cover, just to come about three-quarters up the sides of the dish. Bake for about an hour, until golden and cooked through. The gratin keeps warm well.

Bashed Neeps

Neeps, as swede is known to the Scots, who love to serve this with haggis. The swede has a powerfully peppery flavour, so is best boiled in plenty of water rather than steamed. Don't be mean with the butter and pepper.

Serves 6

1 large swede

Butter

Salt and freshly ground black pepper

Peel the swede and cut into dice. Put in a pan of salted water, bring to the boil and cook for about 20 minutes, until tender. Drain and stir in the butter and lots of freshly ground black pepper. Mash them lightly, then taste and add more salt if necessary.

Chappit Tatties

The archetypal comfort food, mashed potatoes, here enlivened with chopped greenery, are great served with sausages as well as haggis.

Serves 6

1kg potatoes for mashing (Desirée are a good bet)

A teacupful of hot milk

4 tablespoons butter

A small bunch of flat-leaf parsley, chopped

Bunch of spring onions, thinly sliced, including most of the green part

Peel and boil the potatoes in salted water until tender, then drain into a colander and allow to dry for 5 minutes or so, covered with a tea towel.

Return to the pan with the hot milk and mash until really fluffy. Beat in half the butter and then all the parsley and spring onions. Pile into a warmed serving dish and dot with the rest of the butter.

Gnocchi

Homemade gnocchi are better than anything you can buy in a packet, cloud-soft, delicate little morsels. Some recipes include egg, but making them without is no harder, and they will be especially light.

Serves 4 as a main course

500g floury potatoes (Desirée or Maris Piper)

100g plain flour

Boil the potatoes, whole and unpeeled, in salted water until tender. Drain into a colander and cover with a tea towel. Leave to dry for about 10 minutes. Once the potatoes are cool enough to handle strip off the skins.

Mash the potatoes, either through a mouli-légumes or by rubbing them through a sieve. Add enough of the flour, working it in with your fingers to make a soft, still slightly sticky dough.

Generously flour a work surface. Take a tennis-ball sized piece of dough and roll it lightly with your fingertips, shaping it into a long, finger-thick snake. Chop it into 2cm lengths. Repeat with the rest of the dough.

These pieces can be cooked as they are or moulded into the classic shell shape. Take a piece, and, holding a fork in one hand, tines pointing up, press the dough gently on to the base of the prongs to make a dimple. Roll it gently over the prongs so that the undimpled side takes on their impression, then let it drop on the work surface. Repeat with the rest of the gnocchi.

To cook, bring a pan of salted water to the boil. Turn down the heat, and add the gnocchi a few at a time. Once each batch has risen to the surface they can be scooped out with a slotted spoon into a warm, buttered serving dish (a few moments simmering is fine, but if cooked for too long they tend to collapse).

Gnocchi, Butternut Squash, Sage and Shiitake Mushrooms

A happy jumble of autumnal ingredients, this is a good dish when a mixture of vegetarians and meat eaters are coming to supper, since it will satisfy all but the most committed carnivore. I sometimes smarten it up with some extra sage leaves, fried in butter. Frying mellows the somewhat soapy flavour of the herb to an intriguing savouriness, and they have a delicate crispness which is good with the soft squash and chewy mushrooms.

Serves 4

A batch of freshly made gnocchi (see page 169), or around 500g readymade

1 butternut squash (weighing about 800g)

1 tablespoon olive oil

6 sage leaves, shredded

1 garlic clove

120g shiitake mushrooms

Freshly grated Parmesan

Sea salt and freshly ground black pepper

Preheat the oven to 200°C/gas mark 6.

Peel the butternut squash using a vegetable peeler and cut it in half. Scoop out the seeds and fibres. Cut the flesh into chunks the size of a large postage stamp.

Put the chunks in a large shallow baking tray. Drizzle over the oil and toss the chunks until coated, then season with sea salt and grind over black pepper. Roast the butternut squash in the oven for 30 minutes until soft and browned along the edges.

Meanwhile, melt the butter in a large pan. Add the sage and cook for a few seconds until it has deepened in colour. Stir in the garlic, then the shiitake mushrooms. Cook, shaking the pan occasionally, until the mushrooms are edged with gold.

Toss the cooked gnocchi with the mushroom mixture and butternut squash. Serve with the Parmesan sprinkled on top.

To make fried sage leaves

Melt a good dollop of butter in a pan (it should be at a good 1mm deep) and drop in whole sage leaves. Cook until their colour turns bright and the edges begin to brown. Fish out the leaves and leave to cool on kitchen paper. Scatter over the dish just before serving.

Game

I am determined to eat more game. Animals that have lived a free life (or ranged pretty freely in the case of pheasants) are surely a better source of food than miserable factory-farmed animals, or even fairly happy, but constrained well-farmed animals. Even if one doesn't feel disposed to wield a gun oneself, the game-hunting industry gives farmers an incentive to preserve the countryside and wild habitats.

More importantly, game is delicious. The meat has more flavour than most farmed beasts, but it should never taste fetid or overpowering. If you have found game too strong in the past it may well be because it has been hung too long. Hanging is important because it tenderizes the meat and also develops the flavour (pheasant that hasn't been hung can be tough and dull) but it shouldn't be over done. Buy your game from a reputable game butcher and you will be in safe hands as the butcher has no reason to hang animals beyond their best.

Game meat is also healthy, high in iron and low in fat. This last is a double-edged sword. With little or no fat, game dries out easily. So don't be mean with the butter or the streaky bacon.

Guinea Fowl with Porcini and Marsala

Here's a simple casserole taken to new heights with Marsala and dried porcini mushrooms, which give sweetness and a bosky savouriness. If you can't get guinea fowl, use small chickens instead. Either way, eat it with mash or creamy soft polenta, and some purple-sprouting broccoli.

Serves 4

1 guinea fowl, jointed into eight pieces

2 tablespoons plain flour

1 tablespoon olive oil

150ml Marsala

15g porcini, soaked in 400ml boiling water

250ml stock or water

Handful of flat-leaf parsley, leaves only, chopped

Salt and freshly ground black pepper

Pull off the skin from the guinea fowl and discard it: poultry skin goes flaccid when it's casseroled. Season the flour with salt and pepper and turn the guinea fowl pieces in it.

Heat the oil in a large frying pan and brown the pieces on both sides, in several batches. Put them into a heavy-based flameproof casserole, and add the Marsala to the frying pan, stirring and scraping the bits off the base as it boils. Tip into the casserole, along with the porcini, reserving the soaking water.

Strain the soaking water to remove any grit and add to the casserole too, along with the stock or water. Cover and simmer very gently for 40 minutes, until tender, turning the pieces occasionally. Cool and keep in the fridge overnight (or for up to 2 days).

The following day, scrape the fat from the surface and remove the guinea fowl from the pan. Boil the juices to reduce and thicken them to a thin sauce.

To serve, return the guinea fowl to the pan and heat through thoroughly. Taste and adjust the seasoning, tip into a dish and scatter liberally with flat-leaf parsley.

Rillettes

The English name for this dish is potted meat, but as I ate it first in France, it is *rillettes* (pronounced ree-*yet*) to me. Whatever the name, it's the most delicious pâté, little shreds of meat held in a rich, creamy base. Making *rillettes* for the first time takes a bit of effort, but once you have the technique under your belt, there's no looking back.

Wild rabbit is a favourite rillettes ingredient of mine. It's cheap and abundant, and although its dark lean meat can be dry and stringy in casseroles, it's fabulous enriched with duck and bacon fat and potted up like this. (Wild rabbit not available? Then pigeon, duck legs or pork will work well treated the same way.) If you prefer to use your rabbit saddles in another dish, then this is an ideal way to use up the rest. Just use the legs from two rabbits. Likewise, this method works well with duck legs, a more traditional French ingredient, or goose if you are lucky enough to have some spare goose legs. I fancy it would be wonderful, if a little fiddly to make, with pigeon legs.

This is the sort of thing I plonk on the table when friends come round, with hot toast and a saucerful of gherkins, along with some robust red wine. Then I get stuck in along with everyone else. Homemade pâté is a rare treat, and addictively good.

Makes enough to fill a 500ml Kilner jar

1 wild rabbit, skinned, gutted and jointed, or 2–3 duck legs

100g smoked streaky bacon

6 garlic cloves, peeled

2–3 thyme sprigs

Freshly grated nutmeg

Freshly ground black pepper

1 teaspoon salt or 2 teaspoons sea salt flakes

200g duck fat, plus extra to top the pot

Pack the rabbit (or duck) as closely as possible in a flameproof casserole or a slow cooker. Add all the other ingredients along with 150ml of water.

Heat gently until the fat melts, and prod the meat below the surface as far as possible. Cover with a sheet of greasproof paper, pressed onto the surface of the liquid, and a lid. Put into the oven at 150°C/gas mark 2 for 3– 3½ hours, or for 8 hours (or overnight) in a slow cooker. If you are cooking this in the oven, turn the meat every now and then and add more water if it seems to have evaporated. When it is done the meat will be slipping from the bones.

Allow to cool a little. Put a large sieve or colander over a big bowl and pour in the contents of the pan. Pull the meat from the bones, being especially careful to get all the fine rib bones out. Shred the meat with your fingers (don't chop it), fishing out any bones you have missed. Any bacon rind that doesn't squash to a smooth pulp between your fingers should be removed too. Naturally, your hands should be scrupulously clean before you start.

Transfer the meat into another bowl and pour over the fat, (I use a gravy separator), but save the dark juices underneath. If you have more than 4–5 tablespoonfuls, put the juices in a pan and simmer until reduced to that amount. Cool slightly and add to the meat bowl too. Mix, taste and add more salt, pepper, or nutmeg if needed, bearing in mind that the flavour will be more subtle when it is chilled.

Transfer the mix into a pot, bowl or a sterilised Kilner jar. Unless you are planning to eat the *rillettes* in the next couple of days, top with a little more melted duck fat, which will ensure the *rillettes* keep for a week or so. If it suits you better, then transfer to a plastic box and freeze for up to a month.

Duck Breasts with Sweet Potato Purée and Parsnip Crisps

When friends come to supper and I've had a couple of glasses of champagne, I don't want to get all hot and bothered with gravy-making. Dishing up the pink, tender duck with silky sweet potato purée make a sauce unnecessary, and the moreish parsnip crisps take the place of roast potatoes. All you need with this is some steamed purple-sprouting broccoli: cook it beforehand and refresh it in a bowl of iced water. Drain well and reheat just before serving in melted butter. Or forget vegetables and garnish each plate with a posy of deep green watercress.

Serves 6

6 sweet potatoes, unpeeled

1 parsnip

Cooking oil

6 duck breasts (4 if they are
    very large)

Honey

Salt and freshly ground
    black pepper

Preheat the oven to 200°C/gas mark 6. Bake the sweet potatoes for about 40 minutes, until soft and weeping caramel juices. Scrape out the flesh and purée in a food processor, seasoning with pepper and a tiny bit of salt. (This can also be made in advance and refrigerated for up to 2 days.)

Peel the parsnip and use a vegetable peeler to make long, paper-thin strips. In a deep pan, heat the oil (to a depth of about 3cm) until it shimmers. Add the parsnip strips a few at a time, and cook until they just begin to brown. Scoop them out to cool and drain on kitchen paper. Store in an airtight container for up to two days.

Preheat the oven to 230°C/gas mark 8. Rub the duck breast skin with honey and salt and place on a rack over a roasting tin. Leave, covered with a tea towel, to come up to room temperature. Roast the duck breasts for 10–12 minutes, then remove from the oven and leave in a warm place for 10 minutes. Reheat the sweet potato purée in a pan or the microwave. Slice the duck breasts thinly and arrange on plates with the purée and crisps.

Pomegranate

If ever a fruit had a powerful reputation, it's the pomegranate, second only to the apple of mythology. This was the fruit, or strictly speaking, the berry that tempted Persephone to eat in the Underworld, the act which condemned her to spend half of every year in Hell. In Classical and Medieval times the pomegranate was the ultimate symbol of fertility, because of its many seeds and lascivious red interior. Later, it gave its French name – grenade – to a small but vicious explosive device.

The berry itself, a weighty orb with leathery skin and crown-like calyx, has a suitably important look. Inside is the honeycomb of glassy 'arils', garnet beads of juice, each encasing a seed. The bit to be wary of is the creamy yellow pith, which is horribly bitter and tannic.

Use the tangy, juicy, subtly flavoured morsels with creamy, tender food, when the crunch of the seed adds good texture, while the sweet–sour juice is as enlivening as a squeeze of lemon juice. Brown, syrupy pomegranate molasses is the boiled-down version of the juice, which has a gorgeous sour-sherbet flavour.

Releasing the Arils

When I was a schoolgirl, pomegranates were briefly in vogue and we would while away hours carefully extracting the arils one by one with a pin. These days I score the skin deeply around the equator of the fruit, and ease the two halves apart. The arils sit in five segments, and by carefully breaking the fruit apart it is possible to ease them out in clumps. Collect them in a bowl, discard the skin and bitter pith, and wash your sticky hands. The pomegranate is ready to use.

Grilled Aubergine and Lamb with Mint, Feta and Pomegranate

Tangy pomegranate with soft, smoky aubergine, tender lamb and salty feta makes a good lunch or light supper. Try to find Greek or Cypriot feta: it's by far the best.

Serves 4

1 large aubergine, sliced
   pencil thick

Olive oil

8 lamb chops or cutlets

90g feta cheese, preferably
   Greek or Cypriot

Leaves from a small bunch of
   mint, torn

Arils from ½ pomegranate

Salt and freshly ground
   black pepper

Preheat a griddle or grill to very hot. Brush the aubergine slices with olive oil and grill on both sides until browned and cooked through. Sprinkle the lamb with salt and grill or griddle, turning so that the edges brown nicely. Pile on to a plate, and scatter with feta, torn mint leaves and pomegranate. Grind over black pepper and serve.

Rosewater Rice Pudding with Pistachio and Pomegranate

Sweet, milky rice pudding, fragrant with rosewater, gets a real fresh hit from a generous scattering of pomegranate. The pistachios look prettiest if they're skinned to reveal their green interior: just soak them in boiling water for a minute or two and slip off the skins.

Serves 4–6

200g pudding rice or
  risotto rice

1.2 litres milk

6 cardamom pods

4 tablespoons white sugar

2–4 tablespoons rosewater

60g shelled pistachio nuts

Arils from 1 pomegranate

Put the rice in a pan with the milk and whole cardamom pods. Bring to the boil and simmer, stirring occasionally for about 45 minutes, until the rice is swollen and the consistency is porridge-like but not too thick: it will thicken further as it cools. Stir in the sugar and leave to cool, then refrigerate.

Before serving, stir in the rosewater, tasting as you go: rosewaters vary considerably in strength. Scoop into a pretty bowl or bowls and scatter liberally with the pistachios and pomegranate arils.

Other ways with pomegranate

- Cover the top of a cake or cheesecake with the seeds, for example, the Pumpkin Cake on page 141. The crisp, juicy fruit looks beautiful, like glass beads, and is in refreshing contrast to the rich creaminess.

- Put a cupful of couscous in a bowl and cover with a cupful of boiling water. Cover and leave to stand for 10 minutes. Break up the grains with a fork and mix with pomegranate arils, chopped unsweetened dates, chopped parsley and a dressing made from 2 tablespoons lemon juice mixed with 4 tablespoons olive oil. Season with chopped red chilli and salt.

- Mix 1 tablespoon pomegranate molasses with 1 tablespoon olive oil and a good seasoning of salt. Use as a tangy dressing, scattering a few arils over the salad, too.

Chicken with Walnut Pesto and Pomegranate

Walnut and pomegranate is a classic combination, usually in a Middle Eastern *faisinjan*, a pheasant, duck or chicken casserole. This is a simpler version of that partnership, cooked for less time, and using fewer ingredients, but with the same flavour notes. Eat it by itself or with couscous.

Serves 4

4 chicken legs, or 1 whole chicken, jointed

1 tablespoon honey

2 red onions, each peeled and cut into eight wedges, and tossed in a little olive oil

Walnut pesto (see below)

Arils from ½ pomegranate

Salt

Pomegranate molasses (optional)

Preheat the oven to 200°C/gas mark 6.

Rub the chicken with honey and a pinch of salt, and put in a large roasting tin surrounded by the onions in a single layer. Roast for 25 minutes. Serve the chicken and onions with the walnut pesto, and a generous scattering of pomegranate arils, plus a trickle of pomegranate molasses if you have it.

Walnut Pesto

This pesto packs a big flavour punch, earthy, nutty and ferric from the iron-rich parsley. It is good spooned over baked white fish or mixed through pasta as well.

Leaves from a large bunch of parsley

110g shelled walnuts

110ml olive oil

Salt

Put the parsley and walnuts in a food processor with a fat pinch of salt. With the motor running, dribble in the oil, chopping the ingredients coarsely. Stop while it is still a very rough paste. (This mixture will last at least 2 days in the fridge.)

Quinces

Quinces are one of the best of all tree fruits. Their mellow flavour is part apple, part lemony-pear, honeyed and fragrant, and, once you know it, utterly unmistakable. Not that they are much to look at. Yellow and shaped like a knobbly, wonky pear, they are covered in a brown fluff that rubs off easily. This is about the only simple part of quince preparation. Unlike the easy charms of a strawberry or an apple, you have to work for your quincey pleasure.

The fruit is inedible raw, with obdurate flesh, so that cutting it in half seems to require a hatchet. Make do with a strong kitchen knife, and use a vegetable peeler to remove the skin. The core is most neatly and safely removed with a melon baller, but make sure it is a sturdy one. I have broken a couple in the name of poached quinces.

Then you are ready to cook them. The most famous recipe is for *membrillo*, or quince cheese, a thick, jellied sweet paste that is good with cheese (the Spanish famously eat it with Manchego) or nibbled at the end of the meal. Quince can be added to a rich lamb tagine, lending a welcome sour note. I like them best poached first, then made into crumbles, tarts or just eaten with cream.

Cooked in sugar syrup they will soften reasonably quickly, turning a pale pinky-gold. This is how they are often served in restaurants, where they are often disappointing. If you can, allow the quinces to poach for several hours. Dust down your electric slow cooker – it's perfect for this. Eventually the fruit will turn a deep tawny garnet, a carnelian colour. This is a sign that the flavour has mellowed to the characteristic sweet quince, similar to the taste of *membrillo*, and without the acidity of the less well-cooked fruit.

Poached Quinces

The simplest of quince dishes, and worth the time. Once cooked, the quinces can be frozen for 6 months.

450g small quinces

600ml water

280g granulated or
  caster sugar

Peel the quinces with a vegetable peeler. Don't worry if they are a dry brown underneath, but remove any soft brown patches. Halve the quinces and scoop out the core.

Put the quinces in a pan with the peelings and cores, the water and the sugar. Heat gently until the sugar dissolves, then raise the heat and simmer until the fruit is tender. If you want the fruit to turn the distinctive cornelian red, then leave it simmering for several hours, or overnight in a slow cooker.

Remove the peelings and cores and serve the quinces with clotted cream and some of the syrup.

Tip

Leftover syrup can be boiled until it thickens a little, then stored in the fridge. Use it instead of sugar to sweeten apple purée or the fruit for an apple pie, or to brush over a fruit tart to glaze it.

Apple, Pear and Quince Tarte Tatin

If you can't get quinces, you can still enjoy their rich honeyed pear flavour by using quince cheese or *membrillo*, to replace the caramel in a tarte tatin.

Serves 8

50g unsalted butter

2 apples and 2 firm pears, peeled, halved and cored

100g quince cheese or membrillo

100g caster sugar

225g all-butter puff pastry

Melt the butter in an ovenproof frying pan, one about 23cm wide. Add the sugar and quince cheese, mashing it with a wooden spoon to make a smooth gloop. Arrange the apples and pears cut side up on top, alternating in a circle: if they are small, you may have space for another half apple in the middle. Cook over the lowest possible heat for 20 minutes. Remove from the heat and allow to cool for at least 10 minutes, or even overnight.

Preheat the oven to 220°C/gas mark 7. Roll out the pastry to 25cm square and trim off the corners to make an approximate circle. Lay it over the pan, and tuck the edges in round the fruit. Bake in the centre of the oven for 20 minutes, until puffed and deep golden. Allow to cool for a few minutes before inverting onto a plate. (Do this action quickly but carefully because the hot sugar can burn you.) Serve with crème fraîche.

Winter

In winter, more than any other time, I want to be in the kitchen. Warm and fuggy with steam from simmering pots or heat from the oven, it is a welcoming place. We can hunker down and make casseroles, proper puddings, taking a little more time over dishes, without the lure of sunshine outside.

It might seem a dull time of year, but it is far from it. Winter food, deep flavoured, comforting, often beguilingly soft textured, is wonderful, if often underrated. Take cabbage. It's a crying shame that cabbage has such a bad reputation, so much so that it is hard even to say the word without a curl of the lip. Why, when a head of cabbage is such a beautiful thing, blooming like a huge green-petalled peony? We even grow cabbage roses in our gardens, and buy miniature cabbages on stems to make interesting flower arrangements. It probably has much to do with institutional cooking – schools and hospitals – where the smell of boiling cabbage was enough to put off all but the hungriest.

Forget those memories and seek out the January King, its crisp green bowl-shaped leaves touched with purple. Or the Savoy, seersucker-wrinkled leaves, ranging from forest to palest jade colour. Properly cooked, both have a delicate, interesting flavour, and a beguiling nuttiness, as far from school dinners as you can imagine.

Red and white cabbages are less gorgeous to look at, tight balls stripped of their ruff of outer leaves, naked as a skinned rabbit. But the red is good braised to a melting tenderness, with a dash of wine or vinegar to keep the colour bright. Even the chilly-looking white has its charms. Shred it into a fine tangle and toss with brown shrimps as they do at London's St John restaurant, dressing it with olive oil, lemon juice and lots of chopped parsley and chervil.

A few of the tiniest non-pareille capers wouldn't go amiss either. The odd spike added to winter food – capers, lemon juice, chilli, mustard – will keep the tastebuds from hibernating.

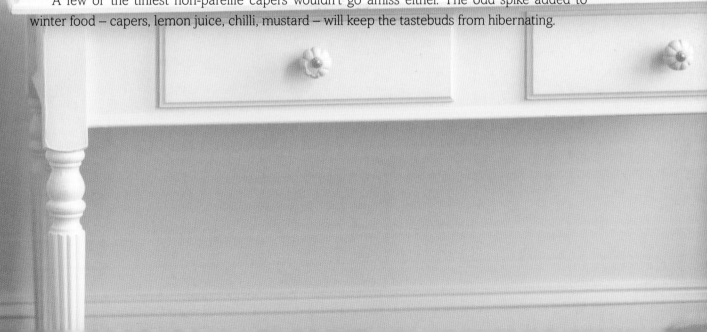

Celeriac

It's not a looker, celeriac, but what it lacks in beauty it makes up for in flavour, gorgeous both cooked and raw. That said, because it browns quickly once cut, I prefer to blanch it in boiling water before using it in a salad, which keeps it clean and pure-looking.

Celeriac, Hazelnut and Tahini Remoulade

Hunt out a Middle Eastern type tahini – Syrian say, or Lebanese – which will have the right silky smoothness. Should there be any wild nuts – cobnuts, filberts or tiny beechnuts – to be had, then use those instead of the hazelnuts. Remoulade is great with cold leftovers or just as a starter with air-dried ham.

Serves 4

1 celeriac

3 tablespoons hazelnut oil

2 tablespoons tahini

Juice of ½ lemon

2 tablespoons roughly chopped parsley

3 tablespoons toasted hazelnuts, roughly chopped

Put a pan of salted water on to boil. Slice off the tough outer layer of the celeriac and cut it into slices 3mm thick. Pile up the slices a few at a time and slice again to make matchsticks. Transfer to a bowl of cold water.

Drop the celeriac into the boiling water and allow the water to come back to a rolling boil, by which time the celeriac should be just about tender. Drain well and stir through the oil and a pinch of salt while still warm. Leave to cool a little, then mix in the tahini and lemon juice. The tahini will stiffen, so add enough water (3–4 tablespoonfuls) to make a coating consistency.

Mix with the parsley and hazelnuts. Taste and check the seasoning.

Apple and Celeriac Waldorf Salad

This is a good winter salad to eat as a starter or with grilled chops. Good-quality rapeseed oil has a deliciously nutty flavour as well as a saffron-yellow colour but olive oil or walnut oil will work as well. Look out for 'wet' walnuts – the fresh new season crop in greengrocers. Beneath the worryingly dirty-looking shell, the nuts are crunchy and delicate.

Serves 4

1 x 500g chunk of celeriac, tough outer layer removed

3 tablespoons rapeseed oil

1 teaspoon cider vinegar

2 sweet apples

1 tablespoon chopped parsley

1 tablespoon roughly chopped walnuts

Put a pan of salted water on to boil. Cut the celeriac into slices 3mm thick. Pile up the slices a few at a time and slice again to make matchsticks. Transfer to a bowl of cold water.

Drain the celeriac matchsticks and add to the pan. Bring back to a rolling boil, by which time the celeriac should be just about tender. Drain well.

In a large bowl, mix the oil, vinegar and a pinch of salt. Add the hot drained celeriac and turn in the dressing. Leave to cool.

To serve, quarter, core and slice the apples and mix into the celeriac with the parsley and walnuts.

Chicory

Satiny white bullets of chicory or *chicons*, as the French call them are a great salad standby in the winter months. Their natural bitterness is mellowed by being grown in the dark, and shielded from the light even after harvesting. (Avoid any with leaves that are edged with green rather than yellow, a sign they have caught too much light, and will be too strong.)

Obligingly, they can wait happily in the salad drawer of the fridge for a week or more, until the occasion demands a quick salad, crisp and mildly bitter. Sweet ingredients work well in the mix, slivers of apple or pear, and a handful of peas (frozen, of course, at this time of year) and some honey in the dressing.

Nor is chicory simply for salads. In Belgium, where it is a favourite, they like to wrap the slender torpedoes in ham and bake them in white sauce. Good, but not as good as the vegetable can be if it is allowed to caramelise a little, the sweetness providing the counterpoint to that bitter edge again, as in the tarte tatin recipe opposite. Also, try halving the chicory heads lengthways, blanching briefly in boiling water, and arranging them around a joint of beef as it cooks. The edges of each cut leaf will darken and crisp in the juices from the roast.

Chicory, Watercress and Pea Salad

Sweet peas from the freezer mellow the bitterness of the crisp, juicy leaves. Lovely with cold meat or after a casserole.

Serves 2–4

1 head of chicory, separated
    into leaves

1 bunch of watercress, coarse
    stems discarded

Handful of frozen peas

½ teaspoon honey

½ tablespoon white wine
    vinegar

2 tablespoons olive oil

Salt and freshly ground
    black pepper

Arrange the chicory and watercress in a bowl. Put the peas in a bowl, pour over boiling water and leave to stand for 5 minutes before draining.

Whisk the honey and vinegar together with a fat pinch of salt and black pepper, then whisk in the oil. Pour the dressing over the salad leaves, turning them well. Spread them on a platter and scatter over the peas. Serve straight away.

Chicory Tarte Tatin

While we think of chicory as a salad vegetable, it's beautiful cooked too, as long as you let it brown to a deep caramel to balance the inherent bitterness. A lovely winter vegetarian starter or main course.

Serves 4

2 tablespoons salted butter

2 tablespoons brown sugar

4 heads of chicory, halved lengthways

1 tablespoon fresh thyme leaves

300g all-butter puff pastry

Parmesan shavings

Preheat the oven to 230°C/gas mark 8.

Melt the butter in an ovenproof 20cm frying pan. Sprinkle over 2 tablespoons brown sugar, then nestle the chicory, cut side down, in a single layer. Cook gently for 30 minutes until browned and tender.

Sprinkle with the thyme leaves. Roll out the pastry thinly and cut a circle slightly larger than the circumference of the pan. Lay over the chicory and tuck in the edges.

Bake for 10 minutes in the very hot oven, then lower the temperature to 180°C/gas mark 4 and bake for a further 20 minutes. Leave to stand for 5 minutes then turn out carefully and serve topped with Parmesan shavings.

Beans and Pulses

We should eat more beans: they are cheap, healthy and delicious. I suspect that many people have been put off by the nut-loaf, hippy-vegetarian associations. The truth is (and I know this will annoy my veggie friends) that by and large, beans are vastly improved by the addition of a bit of meat, transformed from dull and worthy to savoury and delicious. Not much meat, mind – a couple of sausages or rashers of bacon is all that's needed for a pot that serves 4. So, as we worry about the health and environmental implications of too much meat in our diet, but don't want to give up altogether, a bean-rich casserole is a great compromise.

Canned beans are good, and those in jars are better, generally larger and finer quality. Cooking dried is not an option for last-minute suppers, and the cost of the fuel used during the lengthy boiling they require means they're not quite as cheap as they seem. One solution is to use a pressure cooker, which means you can take beans from the packet to the table in 30 minutes – take the Boston baked beans recipe opposite as one example. The downside of pressure cooking is that the beans may break up a bit, but it's a small price to pay, especially if, like me, you like the creamy purée they make.

White Bean and Olive Oil Purée

Much more than the sum of its parts, in this dip-cum-spread the subtle flavour of beans, too often drowned in tomatoes, garlic and bacon, is brought out brilliantly by the olive oil. One to eat with friends, sitting round the kitchen table with a bottle of Italian red, just get them to slather it on toasted bread. Or serve it alongside some simply cooked fish, instead of potatoes.

400g (tinned or home-
   cooked) butter beans,
   drained and rinsed

Extra virgin olive oil

Salt and freshly ground
   black pepper

TO SERVE

Slices of ciabatta, toasted,
   drizzled with olive oil and
   rubbed with garlic

Radicchio or red chicory
   leaves

Purée the beans roughly in a food-processor, adding enough water to make it the consistency of Greek yogurt. Season with salt and pepper, and stir in a tablespoon olive oil.

Pile onto a plate, drizzle with more olive oil, and serve with ciabatta, bruschetta style.

Boston Baked Beans

This recipe for proper American baked beans, sweet and treacly, was originally in the booklet that came with my pressure cooker, but it is so good it is well worth making even if you don't possess one. If you have a slow cooker (another favourite bit of kit) you can transfer it to that at the point where you add the mustard and stock, and cook it slowly for around 4 hours.

You could eat this with sausages but I prefer it on its own or on toast.

Serves 4–6

500g dried haricot beans

2 bacon rashers

2 onions, chopped

4 garlic cloves, chopped

2 teaspoons dry mustard

425ml chicken stock

3 tablespoons molasses or black treacle

2 tablespoons brown sugar

3 tablespoons tomato ketchup

Salt and freshly ground black pepper

Soak the beans overnight (or cook them in a pressure cooker in 1.75 litres of water at high pressure for 2 minutes. Reduce the pressure by running cold water over the lip of the pan.) If you are not using a pressure cooker, place the beans in a large pan with more than enough water to cover and boil vigorously for 10 minutes.

Drain the beans. Chop the bacon and fry it, without adding fat or oil, in the pressure cooker (or a large pan) until browned. Then add the chopped onion and fry until softened. Add the garlic and cook for a further minute.

Stir in the beans, mustard and stock, put on the lid and bring to high pressure. Reduce the heat and cook on high pressure for 6 minutes. (If you aren't using a pressure cooker, add an extra 600ml of water and simmer for 2 hours or more until the beans are tender, topping up the water if necessary.) Allow the pressure to fall naturally, which takes about 10 minutes.

Stir in the molasses or treacle, sugar, ketchup and salt and pepper. Serve up or reheat later – it will be all the better for being kept for a day or two in the fridge.

Beans with Chorizo

This is how I cook beans at home, and a potful will find its way to the table most weeks during the colder months. The meat varies, and might be bacon, belly pork or ordinary sausage, or occasionally lamb. Chorizo is my family's favourite though, ideally the raw 'cooking chorizo', which cooks to a softer texture and gives up more delicious juices to the pot, but the ready-to-eat kind works well too.

Quantities are approximate, since this is eminently adaptable. Go easy on the meat though. It doesn't need much. And another thing – many casseroles improve with keeping, but this one in particular tastes better the next day. Follow it with a cold weather salad or just a bowl of apples.

Serves 4 generously

Olive oil

1 large onion, diced

1–2 garlic cloves, chopped

1kg (approx.) cooked beans (haricot, borlotti or cannellini), from 4 tins or home-cooked

100–200g cooking chorizo, sliced

Chilli sauce (optional)

Salt and freshly ground black pepper

Heat a little olive oil in a pan and add the onion. Cook it slowly until it softens and caramelises (this will take at least 10 minutes).

Stir in the garlic. Cook for a minute or so. Scoop the onion mixture out and set to one side. Add the chorizo to the pan and cook gently until the fat runs. When it begins to colour, splash in a little water and stir well to release all the caramelised gunk on the base of the pan.

Return the onion mix to the pan and add the beans. Pour in enough water to almost cover. Cover and simmer for an hour, until the beans are almost melting. If it seems too runny, remove the lid to reduce the liquid a little.

Season well (the beans need lots of salt), adding a little chilli sauce as well if it needs more kick than the chorizo can give it.

This is very good with toasted white sourdough bread.

Bruschetta with Herb and Cannellini Bean Purée

Toasting bruschetta at the very last minute is a pain, so if you are making this for a party, chargrill the bread in advance instead. It makes for pretty stripes and a smoky flavour which is good at room temperature as well as hot. Top your slices with this creamy, brightly flavoured herb and bean mixture.

Makes 16

1 ciabatta loaf, sliced into
　1cm fingers

Garlic, unpeeled and cut
　in half

Olive oil

Sea salt

FOR THE TOPPING

2 x 400g tins of organic
　cannellini or haricot beans,
　drained and rinsed

4 tablespoons olive oil

2 small bunches of coriander
　and 1 of chervil (or any
　other combination of soft
　green herbs), chopped

Zest and juice of ½ lime

1 red chilli, chopped

Heat a ridged griddle to very hot. Rub the slices of ciabatta with the half garlic clove and brush with olive oil. Cook the bread on the griddle on both sides, pressing down lightly just long enough to make a pattern of charred stripes on the surface.

Mash the beans with 4 tablespoons of olive oil to make a rough purée. Stir in the herbs, lime zest and lime juice, and enough of the red chilli to give it a little kick: taste it and see.

Spread the purée thickly on the bruschetta, dribble a little olive oil over each, scatter with sea salt, and serve.

Mutton with Chilli and Flageolet Beans

Here is one of our staple one-pot supper dishes, called, I regret to say, 'bean slop'. This is a smarter, meatier version than the beans with chorizo, plenty nice enough to give to friends. Follow it with a salad of wiry winter frisée.

Mutton has been unfashionable for decades, perhaps because of memories of strong-smelling, overcooked meat during the austere post-war years. It's coming back into favour now, so we can rediscover its fine flavour. The important thing is to find mutton from farms where the animals have been properly 'finished', which means they will have been fattened up during their final months. Meat that comes from tired old breeding stock will inevitably be tough and dry. Buy from a trusted butcher, in Britain one who is signed up to the Mutton Renaissance Campaign, and you'll be in good hands.

Serves 4

2 tablespoons olive oil

1kg scrag end of neck of mutton or lamb, cut into short lengths but still on the bone

1 large onion, chopped

1 red chilli, chopped

2 garlic cloves, chopped

3 x 400g tins of flageolet beans

400g tin of tomatoes

Sprigs of thyme or rosemary

Salt and freshly ground black pepper

Heat half the oil in a large pan. Add 3–4 pieces of mutton or lamb and brown on all sides. Remove the pieces to a bowl and repeat with the rest of the meat.

Splash a little water into the hot pan and scrape up the gunk on the bottom. Pour the brown liquid into the meat bowl.

Add another tablespoonful of oil to the pan. When it is hot, add the onion and cook until soft. Add the chilli and garlic, and cook for a further minute or so.

Stir in the beans and tomatoes, and nestle in the meat (pouring in the juices too) and herbs. Pour over a mugful of water. Cover and simmer for at least 1½ hours, until the meat is tender.

Remove the lid and simmer until the liquid has reduced to a nice sauce consistency. Taste and season with salt and pepper.

Sweet potatoes

It's all in the name. Sweet potatoes are so sweet that if you bake them whole in the oven, they ooze sticky caramel. Their flesh is honeyed, with a mild spiciness, and an almost fudgey quality. No surprise they are used to make pudding in the United States.

I prefer them simply baked, when they need no butter to enrich them, or puréed to serve with game or duck. They roast well too, although they are best mixed with other vegetables, or they can be too rich.

One caveat: my recipes are for the orange-fleshed sweet potato. The white-fleshed variety are just too mealy and not sweet enough. With their terracotta-coloured skins, it can be hard to tell what you are buying, so if there is no shopkeeper on hand to ask, you will have to scrape a tiny fragment of the skin away to check the colour underneath.

Sweet Potatoes with Angostura Bitters

Angostura bitters are more often found in cocktail bars than in the kitchen. It's worth keeping a bottle at home though, and not simply because a few drops added to tonic water makes a good non-alcoholic drink for drivers.

The rich, mellow taste of sweet potatoes can veer towards cloying, but trickled with carmine bitters it becomes complex and delicious. You could eat these with grilled pork or lamb chops, but it's good enough to make a simple supper with some green veg or fruit to follow.

1 sweet potato per person, unpeeled

Angostura bitters

Put the potatoes on a baking sheet, to prevent sticky juices seeping onto the floor of the oven. The temperature can be varied according to what else you are cooking but think in terms of around an hour at 200°C/gas mark 6.

Once soft, break open and shake in a few drops of angostura. Eat.

Lamb on Rosemary Skewers with Sweet Potatoes and Roast Winter Vegetables

At this time of year, the older tougher stalks of rosemary are just right for lamb kebabs. If you don't have a rosemary bush, then do as I do and sweet-talk a neighbour. Failing that, use a pack from the supermarket, making the holes with a metal skewer first and pushing the soft stems through. The proportions here are vegetable heavy, so up the quantity of meat if you're feeling protein starved.

Serves 2–3

320g carrots, washed and cut into chunks

450g small beetroot, washed and cut into wedges

4 tablespoons olive oil

6 rosemary sprigs

450g lamb leg steaks or neck fillet, trimmed and cut into 3cm cubes

Salt

Preheat the oven to 220°C/gas mark 7. Toss the carrots and beetroot in 3 tablespoons olive oil. Spread them out on a baking tray and roast for 30 minutes.

Thread the lamb on to the rosemary sprigs. Turn them in the last tablespoonful of olive oil and sprinkle with salt.

Preheat a heavy frying pan or griddle and seal the kebabs on all sides until well browned.

Put the kebabs on top of the vegetables and bake for a further 10 minutes or so until done to your liking. Serve with a trickle of oil (some of the herb-flavoured kind if you have it) and couscous or bread.

Other ways with sweet potatoes...

- Use leftover mashed sweet potato instead of pumpkin in the cake recipe on page 141.
- Make sweet potato soup: fry a large, sliced leek in olive oil until soft and add 2 peeled and cubed sweet potatoes and 500ml chicken or vegetable stock. Simmer until soft and purée with a hand blender, adding more water to get a pleasing consistency. Season with salt and chilli and serve with a dollop of natural yogurt.

Oranges, Clementines and Mandarins

We cooks are so lemon obsessed, we can forget about the gentler charms of the orange and its relatives the clementine and mandarin. Lemon glitters and brightens, for sure, but orange has a beguiling quality, a perfumed gentleness that lemon lacks. And, while lemon is very welcome to sharpen oil or spiced dishes, we can eat the flesh of oranges, which is more than can be said for their mouth-puckering yellow sister.

Don't forget that the peel has a resinous charm, like lemon zest but sweeter. It's good mixed through a dish of cooked lentils (puy or continental ones, the kind that hold together when cook rather than falling into a mush) with a vinaigrette and plenty of chopped flat-leaf parsley and chives.

Citrus Fridge Biscuits

A crisp freshly baked biscuit makes all the difference to a pud of shop-bought ice cream. Over Christmas, I keep a roll of uncooked biscuit dough in the fridge (for up to a week) or in the freezer (for a month or more) and just cut off slices and bake them as I need.

Makes about 36

100g butter, at room
  temperature

100g caster sugar

grated zest of 1 clementine,
  1 lemon or ½ orange –
  or a mixture

1 egg

250g plain flour

Salt

In a food-processor or by hand, beat together the butter, sugar and zest until light and fluffy. Whisk in the egg and a pinch of salt. Add the flour and work in gently.

Shape the dough into a log about 5cm thick and wrap well in clingfilm. Leave to firm up in the fridge for at least an hour.

To bake, preheat the oven to 180°C/gas mark 4. Line a baking tray with greaseproof paper.

Cut the dough, straight from the fridge or freezer, into ½cm slices and arrange, well spaced, on the baking tray. Bake for about 12 minutes (the exact time will depend on the thickness of the biscuits) until very lightly coloured.

Lift the hot, still soft biscuits onto a rack to cool and crisp up.

Mandarin Semifreddo with Bitter Chocolate

Cold and creamy, with the sweetness cut by the bitter chocolate, this is a great crowd-pleaser. It's easy to make too, since the joy of a semifreddo is that unlike most ice creams, it doesn't need to be churned as it freezes.

Serves 8–10

5 large eggs, separated

225g caster sugar

Juice of 4 tangerines and grated zest of 2

450ml double cream

TO SERVE

85g dark chocolate, melted

2 mandarins, peeled and sliced (optional)

Line a 1kg loaf tin with a double layer of clingfilm, allowing plenty of overlap.

Put the egg yolks, half the sugar, the tangerine zest and 110ml of the juice (drink the rest) in a heatproof bowl. Rest it over a pan of very gently simmering water and whisk with an electric whisk for 5 minutes, to make a thick, custardy foam.

Take the bowl off the pan and continue to whisk for a further 5 minutes until the mixture has cooled to room temperature.

Whisk the egg whites until stiff peaks form, then whisk in the remaining sugar a spoonful at a time, to make a shiny shaving-foam-like mass. Fold into the egg yolk mix. Beat the cream until thick but still soft and fold that in too.

Scrape the mixture into the lined loaf tin. If there is any left over, it can be frozen in ramekins. Freeze for at least 5 hours.

To serve, turn out the semifreddo and peel off the clingfilm. Cut into 1cm slices and drizzle with melted chocolate. Eat by itself or with slices of tangerine.

Oranges with Saffron

This fruit salad is richly flavoured enough to be really luxurious. It's light and refreshing too, with glorious flame colours.

Serves 8

8 large oranges

3 pinches saffron stamens

1–2 tablespoons white sugar (depending how sweet the oranges are)

Use a sharp serrated knife to peel an orange, cutting away the white inner membrane as well as the skin. Take the wet ball of orange flesh in one hand, and use the knife to carefully cut out each segment from the membrane and remove any pips. (If time's short, just slice the peeled orange.) Repeat with the rest of the oranges.

Spread the orange pieces on a large plate, and scatter with a pinch of saffron. Use a pestle and mortar (or a bowl and the back of a spoon) to crush the sugar and remaining saffron together. Sprinkle over the oranges.

Leave to marinate in the fridge for at least 4 hours or overnight, but remove from the fridge an hour or so before serving, to come up to room temperature.

Chocolate

When I stood in a grove of cacao trees, in the isolated north of the Dominican Republic, the trees were heavy with pods. The shape of a rugby ball and only a little smaller, they grew, bizarrely, straight from the trunk, but they were beautiful, dusky red, ochre yellow and green, the colour variation an indicator of the biodiversity. No GM here, no monoculture, just the farmer choosing to plant seeds from his favourite tree to replenish stock.

José sliced a pod open with his machete to reveal the beans, white on the outside and the purple of a Cadbury's Dairy Milk wrapper within. Around them was a gelatinous pulp, which we sucked from the beans. It tasted of limes and sherbet.

The beans were carried down the potholed track to be loaded into lorries and driven to the cooperative. There they were fermented for five days in wooden cases, then dried on huge racks, carefully turned by hand, before being packed and sent to Europe to be turned into bars. There a whole new process begins, of roasting, grinding and separating, to turn the beans into a molten chocolate soup. It is conched, meaning that it's heated and stirred, for hours, sometimes days, to make it properly smooth, before being set into bars. Chocolate melts at the temperature of our mouths, so it has to be silk-like, with particles tinier than the 20 microns we can detect as graininess.

The result is a food that has almost mythical status. Chocolate is often fêted as 'better than love, sex …' just about anything. And it is good. The problem for the cook, is how to use it, without diluting its charms. After all, what is the point of going to all the trouble of making a pud if it isn't better than just eating a bar of chocolate?

So here, with some trepidation, are my suggestions.

Intense Chocolate Sorbet

This is perfect for when it has to be chocolate for pudding, but the rest of the meal is on the rich side. It delivers a big dark chocolate hit, without much fat. Real chocophiles will want to eat it on its own, or try it with a scoop of vanilla ice cream.

Serves 6

200g granulated or
  caster sugar

100g cocoa

50g dark chocolate

½ teaspoon chocolate
  extract or brandy
  (optional)

Put the sugar and cocoa in a pan with 500ml boiling water. Stir until the sugar has dissolved, then simmer gently for 20 minutes. Stir in the chocolate, chocolate extract or brandy (if using), and a further 200ml cold water. Leave to cool, then churn in an ice cream maker following the manufacturer's instructions. When thick, scrape into a plastic box and freeze.

Transfer from the freezer to the fridge about half an hour before serving in small scoops.

Spanish Hot Chocolate

Spanish hot chocolate is thick and dark, more like a chocolate soup. Traditionally served for breakfast with *churros*, a sort of long doughnut, it's good with the *cañas* on page 208 too, or after dinner instead of pudding and coffee. Put a cinnamon stick on each saucer to stir and flavour it

Makes 2 little cupfuls

300ml milk

1 tablespoon cornflour

1 tablespoon sugar

3 tablespoons cocoa powder

Put all the ingredients in a saucepan and heat, whisking constantly. As it boils it will become thick and creamy. If any lumps form, zap it with a hand blender. Taste and add more sugar if you like. Pour into small tea cups and serve.

Cañas

The Spanish chef and restaurateur José Pizarro's parents, whom I was lucky enough to meet, are both in their seventies and still tend a smallholding of 20 hectares. Señora Pizarro fed me on her homemade *cañas*, crisp curls of flaky cinnamon-scented pastry, which melt richly in the mouth. Gorgeous with coffee or the hot chocolate on page 207.

Makes about 20

125ml olive oil, plus extra
   for deep-frying

Zest of ½ orange

375g plain flour

125ml white wine

125g caster sugar mixed
   with 1 tablespoon ground
   cinnamon

Heat the oil and the orange zest gently in a small pan for 5 minutes.

Put the flour in a large bowl and make a well in the middle. Pour in the hot oil and stir to mix. Add the white wine and mix again. Knead the dough lightly to make a soft, silky, but not sticky dough.

Roll out the dough to a thickness of about 3mm. Cut it in strips 15cm long and 4cm wide.

Heat oil in a pan or wok to a depth of about 5cm (ensure the pan is no more than half full) to 185°C or until a scrap of the dough browns in about 1½ minutes.

Take a cream horn mould or a 12cm length of stainless steel tube, about 3cm in diameter and wrap a strip of dough around it in a spiral.

Put the whole wrapped mould into the hot oil and allow to sizzle for 10 seconds, or until the dough has stiffened and turned pale. With tongs, carefully pull out the metal mould, allowing the spiral of dough to slide back into the oil. Cook for a further minute or so until deep golden.

Carefully lift the spiral out of the oil and drain on kitchen paper. While still warm, dust with the sugar and cinnamon mixture. Repeat with the rest of the dough.

White Chocolate New York Cheesecake

Nothing beats real baked cheesecake, for its dense creaminess, and for the way the texture changes, firmer at the edge, softer towards the centre. Gelatin-set cheesecake is bland and homogenous in comparison. New York cheesecake, deep and with a mild but detectable tang from the cheese, is the best in the world, especially with sweet milky white chocolate in the mix. It needs baking very, very gently if it's not to be stodgy and grainy, but then a recipe like this is one for a peaceful afternoon in the kitchen, not a rush job. I like my cheesecake plain and unadorned, but you could trickle over a little raspberry purée like the one on the strawberries on page 103, or adorn it with the jewel-like seeds from half a pomegranate.

Serves 8–10

16 Oreo® cookies (or use chocolate chip cookies)

3 tablespoons melted butter

600g cream cheese

200g half fat crème fraîche

200g white granulated sugar

20g cornflour

220g white chocolate, melted

½ teaspoon vanilla essence

4 large eggs lightly beaten

First prepare a 20cm springform tin by lining the base with greaseproof paper. Then waterproof it by placing on a large piece of clingfilm and wrap it up the sides of the tin. Repeat with a second piece of clingfilm.

Next make the base: break up the cookies into chunks and blitz them to crumbs in a food-processor. Leaving the motor running, pour in the butter. When well mixed, tip the buttery crumbs into the prepared tin. Press down firmly with your fingers to form an even layer over the base of the tin. Chill in the fridge.

Now for the cheesecake itself. Preheat the oven to 130°C/gas mark ½. Using an electric mixer or food-processor, beat together the cream cheese and crème fraîche. Stir the sugar and cornflour together, and add to the cream cheese mixture. Blend until smooth, then mix in the melted chocolate and vanilla essence. Stir in the eggs – don't beat; you're not trying to add any air here. When they are completely incorporated, pour the mixture into the clingfilm wrapped tin. Boil a kettle full of water. Put the springform tin in a deep roasting tin, and put in the oven. Pour the kettleful of water into the roasting tin, so that the water comes about 3cm up the sides of the springform tin. Bake for 1 hour 10 minutes. At the end of that time, the cheesecake will be slightly browned but still very wobbly – don't worry! Turn off the oven and leave the cheesecake to cool in the oven for 1–2 hours, then remove from its water bath. Stretch clingfilm over the top of the tin and put in the fridge to chill overnight.

To serve, run a knife around the inside of the tin, then remove the outer ring. Ease the cheesecake on to a serving plate using a palette knife or fish slice to help you.

Instant puds

People (I include myself here) are so pleased to be given a pudding, it hardly matters what it is as long as it is sweet. Even a bar of chocolate, broken up and put in the middle of the table, engenders happiness quite out of proportion to the effort. Here are some only slightly more troublesome ideas.

Italian Toast

Dip a slice of panettone in beaten egg and fry in butter until golden. Eat hot with a cool dollop of Greek yogurt, plus apple purée if you like.

Pineapple with Kirsch

Sprinkle pineapple slices with a few drops of kirsch or amaretto. Scatter with pomegranate seeds and serve.

Clementine and Sherry Syllabub

Dissolve 4 tablespoons caster sugar in 2–3 tablespoons sherry (sweet or dry) and mix with the juice and zest of 2 clementines. Whisk 300ml double cream until billowing, then whisk in the sugary liquid. Pour into 4 glasses and chill. Serve with a grating of chocolate and more clementine zest.

Whisky, Black Pepper, Vanilla Ice Cream

Before you choke on your single malt, I'm certainly not suggesting you pour your best whisky, or whiskey, over ice cream. But an everyday blend melds beautifully with sweet vanilla to make a pud that is more than the sum of its parts. A grinding of black pepper adds bite.

Serves 4–6

A tub of good vanilla
  ice cream

Black pepper

Whisky – or whiskey

Scoop vanilla ice cream into tumblers and top with a slug of whisky and a good grinding of black pepper.

Pineapple and Fresh Ginger

I ate this spicy fruit salad on the veranda at the elegantly colonial Eastern & Oriental Hotel in Penang where it was served for breakfast (Malaysians have a sweet tooth). Now I prefer it as a pudding. The spiciness from the ginger increases if you make the salad a day in advance.

100g fresh ginger

225g sugar

1 fresh pineapple

Fresh mint leaves

Peel the ginger, cut it in half lengthways and slice it as thick as a coin. Put the pieces in a pan with the sugar and 300ml water. Heat gently until the sugar dissolves, then boil for 5 minutes or so to make a syrup. Set aside to cool.

Peel, core and slice the pineapple, and put the flesh in the syrup. Allow to marinate for at least an hour. Serve the pineapple scattered with mint leaves.

Bananas in Bubbling Brown Sugar

Heat intensifies the flavour of bananas so they taste almost hyper-real, like banana sweets or banana milk. Bananas in a rich toffee sauce is a gorgeous sugar fix for a cold day.

Serves 4

4 bananas, ripe or unripe, it doesn't matter

50g butter

100g light brown sugar

100ml single cream

Squeeze of lemon juice

Preheat the oven to 200°C/gas mark 6.

Halve the bananas lengthways and lay them in an ovenproof dish that just fits them in a single layer.

Melt the butter and mix in the brown sugar, cream and lemon juice. Pour over the bananas and bake for 20 minutes until the sauce is thick and bubbling. Eat with extra cream or ice cream.

Winter Parties

Winter drinks parties, dark outside, candles inside, are fantastically atmospheric. Warm and snug, plenty to drink – no wonder they always seem to go on much longer than planned. Which means that there must be food, and plenty of it, to soak up the booze.

Avoid nuts and crisp, which are so salty they just make you thirstier, and in any case smack of cheap bars. Little things to eat – canapés, for want of a better word – are ideal, and terribly impressive. They make guests feel cosseted, too, worth the effort. Hot canapés are easiest, since they can often be made in advance and heated through or baked. That means being in the kitchen, but then even cold canapés quickly look tired, and generally need last-minute attention. Make it easy on yourself, though – rather than attempting to put a tiny herb leaf on every canapé, just strew lots of fresh leaves over the whole plate before handing it round. And don't even think of trying to tie a chive round a smoked salmon parcel.

That said, there is no getting away from the fact that party food is a fiddle. Is it all worth it? To me, yes. I love the miniaturist detail that canapé-making demands, and I even like an excuse to hole myself up in the kitchen rather than circulating. But if you don't enjoy it, go to the deli instead, and buy enough really good cheese and charcuterie to cover a huge board.

Now to be bossy. This kind of food does bring out my inner Fanny Cradock, but listen up, even if it sounds fussy.

- Do make sure the canapés are really little, generally the size that can be eaten in one mouthful. As soon as something has to be bitten into, there is a risk that it'll burst, or crumble, or just fall apart – which makes people look clumsy, which they hate. Definite downer.
- Avoid dripping, staining sauces for the same reason. (I was once given satay with a turmeric-laced peanut sauce, and my hostess still has the marks on her sofa to show for it.)
- Think twice about dips at big parties partly for the reason above and partly because they are (sorry) harbourers of bacteria, dangerous if you have pregnant or elderly guests.
- Hand round cocktail napkins at the same time as the canapés. I might be happy to wipe my hands on my skirt but not everyone is.
- Have a pot on hand for discarded sticks and pits.

Quick party food

- **Teacups of soup** (such as the pea and parsley on page 52 – purée it to make a smooth texture) are warming and can be managed with a glass in the other hand.
- **Figs and prosciutto** – wrap fig eighths in strips of prosciutto, tucking in a leaf of basil.
- **Mini poppadoms with raita and mango chutney** – buy bags of mini poppadums and top with a tiny dollop of bought raita or tzaziki and another of mango chutney.
- **Cocktail sausages** – always have cocktail sausages. Easy to cook (toss them in honey and grain mustard before baking if you want to be fancy) and universally popular.
- **Smoked salmon, dill butter** – in the food-processor, blitz a bunch of fresh dill with 50g butter and a squeeze of lemon juice. Spread on pumpernickel bread and cover with slices of smoked salmon. Trim with a sharp knife and cut into neat dominoes. Grind over black pepper and scatter with more dill fronds before serving.

Lamb, Feta and Roast Tomatoes

Everyone loves this savoury, intensely flavoured canapé. They are a little soft to pick up, so rest each tomato on a ready-made crostini. Once cooled, the tomatoes can be stored in the fridge for up to 2 days.

Makes 16

8 tomatoes

200g lamb neck fillet (or lamb steak)

2 teaspoons honey

2 teaspoons oil

1 small garlic clove, crushed

Few drops of chilli sauce

50g Greek feta cheese

Fresh mint leaves

Preheat the oven to 150°C/gas mark 2.

Cut the tomatoes in half horizontally and lay out, cut side up, on a roasting tray.

Cook for about 2 hours, until wrinkled and slightly dried. Allow to cool.

Trim excess fat from the lamb fillet and cut it into 16 slices. Mix together with the honey, oil, garlic and chilli sauce. Marinate for at least 30 minutes.

Fry the lamb in a hot pan until just browned on both sides.

Put a piece of lamb on each tomato. Heat through in the low oven. (You can make these up to 30 minutes before serving.)

Just before serving, crumble over the feta and sprinkle with mint leaves.

Hot Smoked Salmon Fishcakes

A little bit of spice does wonders for a fishcake – these are good made full-size for lunch, too, to eat with salad and a dollop of mayonnaise. Use smoked salmon or poached fresh salmon to make these fishcakes if you prefer.

Makes 16–18

1 tablespoon butter

Pinch of turmeric

½ teaspoon grated fresh ginger

175g floury potatoes, boiled and mashed

Small bunch of flat-leaf parsley

Chilli sauce

1 small egg, lightly beaten

100g hot smoked salmon, flaked

Flour, for dusting

Vegetable oil, for frying

Salt and freshly ground black pepper

Small pot of crème fraîche mixed with 3–4 chopped spring onions, to serve

Melt the butter and add the turmeric and ginger. Allow to bubble for a few seconds before mixing with the potatoes. Finely chop half the parsley leaves and mix into the mash. Taste and season with a little salt and lots of pepper plus a splash of chilli sauce. Beat in enough of the egg to make a soft but not loose consistency. Stir in the salmon flakes.

Put about 2 tablespoons flour in a bowl and drop in a teaspoonful of the mixture, rolling it into a ball. Repeat with the rest of the mixture, flattening each ball slightly. Transfer to a plate and cover. Refrigerate for at least an hour, and up to a day.

To cook, heat the oil in a frying pan to a depth of ½cm. Cook the fishcakes on both sides until golden. (This could be done an hour ahead and the fishcakes reheated in a hot oven.)

Top each fishcake with a sprig of parsley. Serve with the crème fraîche and spring onion dip.

Slow Roast Rosemary Pork Belly with Blue Cheese

Sweet-savoury pork belly with the bite of salty-bitter cheese makes for a big flavour. They are filling, too, great for a drinks party where canapés are taking the place of a proper meal. For two canapés in one, chop the pork crackling into strips and serve with a bowl of apple sauce for dipping, just as Mark Hix does at his Soho restaurant.

Makes 10 or so

500g pork belly, unrolled

Sprigs of rosemary

50g blue cheese

2 teaspoons redcurrant jelly

Salt and freshly ground
 black pepper

Preheat the oven to 140°C/gas mark 1.

Score the pork skin in long lines 1cm apart, cutting through the skin but not the fat. Use a razor sharp knife or a craft knife for this.

Take a large sheet of foil and lay the rosemary sprigs in the middle. Season the pork belly with salt and pepper and put it on top, skin side up. Scrunch the foil around the sides of the pork, leaving the skin uncovered.

Bake for 4 hours until very tender. Leave to cool. Carefully slice the crackling off the pork, leaving behind as much fat as possible. Wrap the pork tightly and keep in the fridge for up to 3 days.

To assemble the canapés, heat a large frying pan and put the pork in, fat side down. Cook gently until the fat is golden and the pork is hot through.

Cut the pork into squares or rectangles. At this point they can be wrapping in foil and kept warm in a low oven for an hour or so.

Just before serving, top with a sliver of blue cheese and a tiny button of redcurrant jelly.

Pork Crackling Twigs with Apple Sauce

2 large cooking apples,
 peeled, cored and chopped

2 cloves

Sugar

Skin from the belly pork

Put the apple pieces in a pan with the cloves and 2 tablespoons water. Cover and cook gently until the apples are collapsing, adding a little more water if it threatens to catch.

Taste the apple mix and add enough sugar to balance the acidity, without making it too sweet – it's not a pudding.

Heat the grill to medium high and cook the pork skin underneath until it puffs up, watching carefully that it doesn't burn. Break it into strips. (This can be done 3–4 hours ahead.)

Serve the pork crackling with the warm apple sauce.

Manchego, Quince Cheese and Toasted Almonds

Manchego and *membrillo* (quince cheese) is a classic combination, but one that's improved by the crunch and flavour of toasted almonds.

Makes 20 or so

150g Manchego cheese

150g *membrillo* (quince cheese)

100g blanched almonds

Preheat the oven to 200°C/gas mark 6.

Spread the almonds on a baking tray and bake for 5–10 minutes until golden. Remove and set aside to cool.

Slice the cheese and *membrillo* into squares or triangles about ½cm thick. Lay a piece of *membrillo* on top of each piece of cheese.

Press an almond into each piece. Keep covered in the fridge for up to a day.

Masala Spiced Popcorn

Curry spice turns popcorn a crocus-yellow colour with a gentle flavour that's addictive. Use any curry paste or powder and serve in bowls or make little greaseproof paper cones to hand round.

Enough for 8 little cones

30g popped popcorn

30g butter

1 teaspoon Masala curry powder or paste

Fresh dill or coriander leaves

Melt the butter in a large pan and stir in the curry powder. Cook gently for a minute, then tip in the popcorn.

Remove the pan from the heat and stir well until the popcorn is well coated. Taste and add a little salt.

Serve with dill or coriander scattered over.

More drinks party rules

- Site drinks at the back of the room to encourage people in and prevent a bottleneck at the entrance.
- If you have invited more than eight people (12 if you are a couple) you will need help. Enlist friends to answer the door, take coats and serve drinks, or hire staff, either professionals or friendly teenagers.
- Allow a dozen canapés a head for an all-evening party, four for pre-dinner.
- Canapés look better if there is just one kind on each plate. It also means servers can move round the room faster, without hold ups as people decide which canapé to choose.
- Don't overload the serving plate. Depending on the size of the party, 8–16 canapés at a time is plenty. That way they stay looking fresh.
- Refill the platter when only two or three canapés remain. Hawking round a last canapé is a dispiriting experience.

Mini Croissants with Mushrooms and Thyme

Dear little tiny croissants can be filled with whatever you like – I use mushrooms here but cheese and ham would work well too. Make your filling well flavoured though, as you'll only be able to fit a miniscule amount inside. The best thing is that these can be made a month in advance and frozen, unbaked, on trays, then packed into airtight boxes. Bake them straight from frozen, just giving them an extra 2–3 minutes.

Makes 24

30g butter

½ onion, finely chopped

225g mushrooms (include some dried, soaked porcini if you can), finely chopped

1 small garlic clove, crushed

Leaves from 2 good thyme sprigs

1 packet of croissant dough (available as a tin in the chill cabinet of large supermarkets)

Beaten egg

Poppy seeds (optional)

Preheat the oven to 200°C/gas mark 6.

Melt the butter and fry the onion for 5 minutes, until softened. Add the mushrooms, garlic and thyme and cook until all the liquid from the mushrooms has evaporated. Season well and set aside to cool.

Open the tin of croissant dough and peel off one triangle of dough. Roll it out on a lightly floured surface until the triangle measures about 28 × 13cm. Cut off the tip about halfway down to make one small triangle, and divide the rest into three further triangles.

Place ¼ teaspoon of mushroom mixture at the broad end of one triangle, and roll it up towards the central point. Make sure the point is well stuck down and pull the tips firmly round to the front to form a croissant shape. They tend to straighten as they bake so the curve should look exaggerated. Repeat with the rest of the dough and place on a greased baking tray.

Brush with beaten egg and sprinkle with poppy seeds if you like. Bake for 10–12 minutes until golden brown, and serve warm.

Index

Acknowledgements

Judith Hannam, my editor, has been patience in the face of my endless prevarications and periods of ostrich-like behaviour, dealing with them with graciousness and humour. I am in awe of her ability to nudge a book into shape with tact and just the occasional pithy comment. Thank you Judith.

I'm also so grateful to Kyle Cathie for her wisdom, forbearance and kindness. Kyle is a remarkable publisher to write for, and it has been a privilege.

Thank you to Caroline Michel, my warm, elegant agent, who brought Kyle and me together.

Hugs all round for the women who made the book look so fabulous. Tara Fisher, your photographs, as always, are luminous, Annie Rigg the styling is exactly right, and Jacqui Caulton, the design is faultless. Thank you all.

Samuel Goldsmith, friend and assistant, thank you for all your help and encouragement, for testing recipes and for nagging me.

Last, but largest, thanks to my family, to my son Hector and daughter Campaspe who had to live with a mother who was even more distracted than usual for so many months. And especially to my husband Richard, who supports me even when I am insupportable, and above all believes in me.